# *Introduction*

## About the Play

### *Love or duty?*

She's not fourteen! Juliet's father isn't sure that she is old enough to be married. But Paris, eager to make her his wife, insists that other girls of Juliet's age in Verona who are already 'happy mothers'. And Lady Capulet, who gave birth to Juliet at fourteen, raises no objections. And Juliet? She hasn't given much thought to the subject ('It is an honour that I dream not of'), but she's an obedient child, and she promises to give serious consideration to the man her parents have found for her.

And then she meets Romeo.

He's the last man they would have chosen. He's a Montague—the son of their oldest enemy. The quarrel between the two families has been going on so long that nobody can remember how it started. Juliet knows something about it, of course—but does it matter? What's in a name? Romeo would still be the man she loves, whatever his name: 'a rose/By any other word would smell as sweet'.

### *Shakespeare's sources*

This is one of the oldest and best loved stories in the world: two young lovers, little more than children, cannot understand the hatred of an older generation that keeps them apart, and choose to die together rather than live without each other. It has been traced as far back as the third century AD[1], and it became popular in Europe in the fifteenth century when Italian writers began to give it details which we can now recognize in Shakespeare's play. They claim the story was contemporary and factual—so successfully that even today tourists in Verona can be shown the balcony and tomb of Giulietta.[2]

Shakespeare found the story in a narrative poem, *The Tragicall History of Romeus and Juliet* by Arthur Brooke. He adapted it for his own audiences, making Brooke's sixteen-year-old Juliet much younger, and more dependent on her Nurse—whose role and character are

---

[1] In the *Ephesiaca* of Xenophon of Ephesus.

[2] The two families involved in the action are historical: the Montecchi lived in Verona, and the Capelletti in nearby Cremona, and Dante speaks of them (*Purgatorio* VI) as being partly responsible for the civil strife in thirteenth-century Italy.

richly extended. Brooke allows his Romeus and Juliet three months of married happiness, but Shakespeare, speeding up the action, permits them just one single night of wedded bliss.

### Different attitudes

The two authors have very different attitudes to their subjects. Brooke, although he describes the situations with relish, openly disapproves of the conduct of Romeus and Juliet, whom he describes as

> a couple of unfortunate lovers, thralling themselves to unhonest desire, neglecting the authority and advice of parents and friends, conferring their principal counsels with drunken gossips . . . attempting all adventures of peril for the attaining of their wished lust [and] abusing the honourable name of lawful marriage . . . [3]

Shakespeare, by contrast, is tender—often amused but always sympathetic. His understanding extends beyond the characters of his hero and heroine, and includes the Nurse—talkative, bewildered, panic-stricken; Romeo's friend Mercutio, who is as quick with his sword as with his tongue; and even Friar Lawrence who, although things go sadly wrong, is motivated by the best intentions in the world—to make peace, and to use love to conquer hate.

### Creating characters

No other dramatist of this period creates characters in quite the way that Shakespeare does: while other writers create stereotypes, Shakespeare creates individuals. Their vitality comes in part from the precise information we learn about them—information which is unnecessary to the plot of the play: we do not *need* to know that the Nurse's daughter was called Susan, or that her husband was 'a merry man', but details like these make the character come alive. In addition, Shakespeare's characters show subtle differences in the way they speak, just as real people do. The rhythms of the Nurse's speeches are quite different from those of Mercutio's explosive outbursts, and these again are unlike Benvolio's solemn utterances.

Shakespeare takes even greater care with his central characters. Romeo's witty introspection when he is describing his passion for Rosaline, the first lady he has fallen for, sounds very different from the quiet eloquence with which he speaks his love for Juliet. In the balcony

[3] From a prose address 'To the Reader' at the beginning of his poem.

scene Shakespeare shows the change *as it is happening*, when Romeo hesitates between his former rhetoric ('It is the east, and Juliet is the sun') and his new-found simplicity—

> It is my lady, O it is my love:
> O that she knew she were!

Romeo seems to grow older as the play progresses, and the verse reflects and expresses the change in his character. The same is true of Juliet, who matures from docile child-bride to determined tragic heroine in the course of the five acts.

### A time of change

It is rarely possible to give a precise date for plays written in the sixteenth and seventeenth centuries, but it is generally agreed that this one was written around 1594–96—at much the same time as *A Midsummer Night's Dream*, where the interlude of 'Pyramus and Thisbe' might almost be a parody of *Romeo and Juliet*. Shakespeare seems to have been intensely active during these middle years of the decade, when poets and dramatists alike were experimenting with a variety of styles: blank verse was a fairly new form, and so was the sonnet, and the English language lent itself to every kind of manipulation. Shakespeare is willing to try his hand at all of them, matching the excitement of his plot with a display of formal variations and verbal fireworks. The action includes the tensions of hot-blooded sword-play, romance by moonlight, and bawdy comedy in the marketplace; the style flows from prose to verse; and the language ranges from passages of great lyrical beauty to puns and bawdy jokes.

### Challenges and solutions

Shakespeare's mind was overflowing with ideas and images. He had read a great deal—modern and classical poetry (both in Latin and in English translation), popular fiction and serious prose works (including the Bible), and he knew the plays of contemporary and earlier dramatists. But he was also a skilled craftsman with a working knowledge of the resources and limitations of the theatre in which his play would be performed. With two acting levels, he could plan for balcony scenes, and since there was no fixed scenery and nothing to interrupt the action, he could allow characters to change places (from Verona to Mantua, from street to bedroom) without any break in the movement of the play—although he had to always take care to write a reference to the place into someone's speech, so that the audience does not get lost. All performances in the public theatres took place in daylight—so for the night scenes Shakespeare makes sure that at least one character mentions the stars, the moon, or the torches that the actors are carrying.

### A source of inspiration

*Romeo and Juliet* has always been one of Shakespeare's most popular plays. In the twentieth century it has been given a variety of different treatments, ranging from the traditional (doublet and hose) to the contemporary (red sports car and high-powered motor bike in Verona square). The story has been adapted to make great ballets, and in 1956 Jerome Robbins turned it into the musical *West Side Story*, setting it in New York's Spanish Harlem, where the quarrel was between rival gangs, the Jets and the Sharks (Americans and Puerto Ricans), and the Prince of Verona was a harassed police lieutenant. Shakespeare's text (with some drastic cutting) was the script for a recent film by Baz Luhrman, which illuminated some tired metaphors with daring visual puns, and demonstrated that there is nothing sacred about the iambic pentameter when it is spoken quite naturally in 'Verona Beach' (California), where the fighting is with 'Sword 9mm' guns, Captain Prince patrols his territory in a helicopter, and Romeo courts Juliet whilst they swim in her father's pool.

# Leading Characters in the Play

**Escales**  Prince of Verona. Although he must try to be impartial, he is not indifferent to the feud between the Montagues and the Capulets, because he has relatives on both sides.

### The Montague family

**Montague and Lady Montague**  Romeo's parents, who are still active in an old feud with the Capulet family.

**Romeo**  Their only son, a romantically-inclined young man desperately in love with a lady called Rosaline—until he meets Juliet, the daughter of his family's enemy.

**Benvolio**  One of Romeo's friends, a serious and sensitive young man whose name (= good will) indicates his peace-making role.

**Mercutio**  Romeo's other friend, whose aggressive vitality (shown in speech as well as action) provokes a duel—with a tragic outcome that affects every character in the play.

### The Capulet household

| | |
|---|---|
| **Capulet and Lady Capulet** | Juliet's parents, who are anxious that their daughter should make a socially advantageous marriage. Juliet's father will not tolerate disobedience, and her mother (perhaps opting for a quiet life) puts her husband's will before her daughter's wishes. |
| **Juliet** | Their only child (other children have apparently died). Juliet is almost fourteen years old and seems happy enough to obey her parents—until, quite by chance, she meets Romeo. |
| **Tybalt** | Juliet's cousin, a sophisticated and fashionable young man who is proud of his own accomplishments, and very jealous of the family honour. |
| **Juliet's Nurse** | An affectionate, simple-minded woman in whom piety and sexuality are combined with commonsense and a desire to please. She breast-fed Juliet as a baby, and has been looking after her ever since. |
| **Paris** | A nobleman, endowed with all the qualities that would make him (in her parents' eyes) an ideal husband for Juliet. |
| **Friar Lawrence** | A friar of the Order of Saint Francis, whose good intentions precipitate the tragedy. |

# Synopsis

## ACT 3

SCENE 1   Mercutio, outraged when Romeo refuses Tybalt's challenge, draws his own sword, and in the fighting that follows both he and Tybalt are killed. Romeo is banished from Verona.

SCENE 2   Juliet is eagerly waiting for her husband, but the Nurse brings bad news.

SCENE 3   Friar Lawrence tries to console Romeo and find a solution for the problems.

SCENE 4   Juliet's father makes plans for her to marry Paris.

SCENE 5   It is already dawn, and Romeo must leave Juliet. Their parting is interrupted by the Nurse, who gives warning that Juliet's mother is looking for her daughter. Lady Capulet brings news of the arranged marriage.

## ACT 4

SCENE 1   Friar Lawrence has a plan to save the situation.

SCENE 2   The Capulets are preparing for the wedding. Juliet assures her father that she will obey him, but the wedding day is changed.

SCENE 3   Although she is frightened, Juliet takes the Friar's drug.

SCENE 4   The Capulet household prepares for the wedding, and the Nurse goes to wake Juliet.

SCENE 5   Juliet cannot be woken; the whole family join together to lament.

## ACT 5

SCENE 1   In Mantua, Romeo hears news of Juliet's death.

SCENE 2   Friar Lawrence learns that Romeo has not received his letter and hurries to the Capulets' vault.

SCENE 3   Paris, praying at Juliet's tomb, encounters Romeo; they fight, and Paris is killed. Friar Lawrence is too late to save Romeo, who swallows the poison he bought in Mantua, and when Juliet sees his body she kills herself. Friar Lawrence explains everything.

## *Romeo and Juliet*: Commentary

Most of the play takes place (as the Chorus explains) in 'fair Verona'—
an attractive little city in the north of Italy. The action moves swiftly
from the city streets to the hall of Capulet's house, to the orchard below
Juliet's balcony, to Friar Lawrence's lonely cell, and finally to the vault
where the ancestors of the Capulets are entombed. The Elizabethan
stage had no curtains, and of course the theatre sold no programmes, so
the characters themselves tell us where they are. They even indicate the
time of day. The play starts on a Sunday morning in the middle of July;
less than five days later—just before dawn on the following Thursday—
it is all over.

### Prologue

The Chorus—a single figure—appears on stage. He is not a character
and has no personality. His function is simply to explain the situation,
telling us that we are now in Verona, and that this is a city divided by
civil war between two noble families. Their quarrel is an old one, an
'ancient grudge'. We never learn its cause: it seems to have become a
habit for the Capulets and the Montagues to hate each other. But if we
cannot know the cause of the quarrel, we can be warned of its cure.

When Shakespeare wrote *Romeo and Juliet* it was not unusual for a
dramatist to introduce his play in this manner. The words of the Chorus
would silence a restless audience, and settle the spectators into an
appropriate mood for the first scene.

### Act 1

Scene 1    Sunday morning. It is not yet nine o'clock, and two of Capulet's
servants, Sampson and Gregory, have nothing very much to do as they
wander through the streets of Verona. They tease each other, but when
they see two of Montague's servants approaching, their good-natured
rivalry is converted to hostility. All the servants are cowards, however,
and can only exchange rude words and gestures until Benvolio's arrival
gives the Montague servants confidence. Then Sampson issues the first
challenge: 'Draw, if you be men'. Benvolio's attempts to make peace are
frustrated by the arrival of Tybalt; at once the young noblemen are
engaged in the fighting. Citizens of Verona rush to take sides, some
urging a truce, some encouraging the Montague faction, and others

joining the Capulet party: 'Strike! Beat them down! Down with the Capulets! Down with the Montagues!' Immediately the heads of the two families appear on the scene. Capulet calls for his 'long-sword'—a heavy, old-fashioned weapon that would have had no effect against the modern rapiers used by the younger generation. For a moment the two wives, Lady Capulet and Lady Montague, try to restrain their husbands, but their efforts are unnecessary. The Prince has arrived.

Escales, Prince of Verona, is the representative of law and order in the play. His commands are obeyed, and his threats disperse the crowd. But we have seen enough to realize the gravity of the situation. In fewer than a hundred lines Shakespeare has created an atmosphere of tension where the least word or gesture can trigger off unthinking violence. That violence is shared by the entire community—old and young alike, whether they are the lowest servants or the respected heads of noble families.

With the departure of the Prince, the mood of the scene changes. Lady Montague asks the question that the audience wants to ask: 'O where is Romeo? Saw you him today?' We have seen war; and now we hear about love, as Benvolio describes the behaviour of his infatuated friend. Romeo is up before dawn, walking alone in the woods and weeping; when the sun rises, he hurries home, locks himself in his room, and shuts out the daylight. These are the early symptoms of unrequited love, although neither Benvolio nor Romeo's parents appear to recognize this.

We wait for Romeo to show us the extent of his love-sickness. Romeo is miserable—we can have no doubt about that. We can be equally sure, however, that he *enjoys* his misery. He knows that there has been some kind of disturbance in the streets, but he is not interested. What matters to Romeo is the emotion that he calls 'love'. It makes him happy—and at the same time it makes him sad. He tries to express these two conflicting states in a series of witty paradoxes—phrases which seem absurd, and where the meaning of one word contradicts the sense of the word to which it is linked:

Feather of lead, bright smoke, cold fire, sick health.

He expects Benvolio to be amused, but Benvolio is a solemn young man and offers sympathy to his friend. Romeo welcomes the sympathy: it gives him an opportunity to talk even more about himself and his feelings—and this gives us the information that we need about his state of mind.

Romeo believes himself to be in love, but the woman he loves is not interested in him. He describes her to Benvolio and tells us that she is perfect; but we can learn no more. (In the next scene we discover that her name is Rosaline and that she is a Capulet.) We can safely conclude, however, that this is only a young man's fancy, and a kind of sickness that could probably be cured if Romeo would follow Benvolio's prescription and 'Examine other beauties'.

He will soon be able to do this.

SCENE 2    Capulet has returned home after his talk with the Prince, and he seems to be reconciled to the idea that he and Montague should start to live at peace with each other. He has important business to deal with. The County Paris is eager to make Juliet his wife. Capulet is a *good* father and Juliet is his only child. There have been other children, but they are dead: 'Earth hath swallow'd all my hopes but she'. This must make Juliet very precious to him and he is reluctant to lose her. However, if she should fall in love with Paris, her father will be happy to give his consent to the marriage.

That evening (it is still Sunday) Capulet will hold 'an old accustom'd feast'—an elaborate ball which will be attended by all the nobility of Verona. It is a regular event, and the message that Capulet now sends to his guests is probably not so much an invitation as a reminder.

The servants in the first scene speak in plain, simple prose. Benvolio and Tybalt speak a flexible blank verse—that is to say, verse where the regular stresses of the iambic pentameter fit in with the formal rhythms of speech. Prince Escales, coming on to the stage at line 75, speaks a much more dignified blank verse; his is the kind of speech that is delivered from a platform. Romeo uses rhymes when he speaks of the nature of his love: the subject is 'poetic', and so it is appropriate that the verse should seem equally unreal—remote from everyday speech. In the second scene there is always a tendency for the lines to rhyme in couplets, and the effect is to speed up the action: it is important that we should know about the feast, but there is no need for us at the moment to pay very close attention. The servant who carries Capulet's invitation speaks in prose, but not the same kind of prose as that spoken by Sampson and Gregory in the first scene, and Shakespeare's contemporaries would recognize this passage as being a parody of a kind of ornate prose that was fashionable in the last decade of the sixteenth century. It is a comic moment, and the scene continues with comedy (often with rhymed couplets) as Romeo and Benvolio learn about the Capulet ball and Benvolio makes a suggestion.

SCENE 3    The couplets give way to blank verse again as the scene changes once more. We are inside the Capulet house again, this time awaiting an introduction to Juliet. She stands quiet and obedient whilst her Nurse—the foster-mother who has cared for her since the day that she was born—remembers incidents in the child's life. At the beginning of the scene Lady Capulet dismisses the Nurse: 'Nurse, give us leave awhile. We must talk in secret.' But immediately the Nurse is recalled: 'Nurse, come back again. I have remember'd me, thou's hear our counsel.' The Nurse, we realize, is not an ordinary servant; she is almost a member of the family. When she begins to tell us about Juliet's childhood we learn not only Juliet's age (although this is very important) but also a great deal about the character of the Nurse. She has known personal sorrow in the death of her daughter, Susan, but she is philosophical about this: 'Well, Susan is with God, She was too good for me.' She remembers trivial details, her speech is repetitive, and she cannot continue a line of thought for very long. Lady Capulet is a complete contrast. She asks a direct question: 'Tell me, daughter Juliet, how stands your dispositions to be married?' Juliet's answer is evasive: 'It is an honour that I dream not of'; after all, she is not yet fourteen. But her mother persists: 'Well, think of marriage now'. She introduces the subject of Paris and his proposal of marriage. Her description of Paris is no doubt intended to recommend the gentleman to her daughter, but the extended metaphor (spread over eleven lines of verse) has no effect upon *our* emotions. Juliet's reply shows only a young girl's obedience.

The arrival of the servants with the information that 'the guests are come', breaks into the strained formality, and we are made aware that time has been passing. It is now Sunday evening. Lady Capulet responds to the servant's request and leaves the stage in order to receive her guests at supper. She is followed by Juliet and the Nurse.

SCENE 4    Their departure does not leave the stage empty for long. Romeo enters (at the opposite side of the stage) accompanied by Mercutio and Benvolio, with a few other companions. They are all disguised— wearing fancy dress and comic masks to hide their faces. Attendants bear torches, and there are probably musical instruments—certainly there is a drum (line 114). Benvolio has organized a *masquerade*—an amateur entertainment, fashionable in the sixteenth century, in which gentlemen could visit a party to which they had not been invited. After making a speech to the host (the speech referred to by Benvolio in the first line of the scene), the strangers would dance, flirt with the ladies,

pay compliments to the host, and then depart. The host regarded the arrival of masquers as a form of flattery, not in any sense an intrusion into the privacy of his party.

Throughout the scene we are constantly made aware of the fact that it is dark; night has fallen, and torches must be used to give the illusion of darkness. Benvolio and Mercutio are full of enthusiasm for the masquerade, but Romeo is reluctant to join them. He would prefer to be alone with his love-sick misery—and he has a strong sensation of impending disaster: 'I dream'd a dream tonight'. But before Romeo's dream can threaten to spoil the light-hearted fun of the scene, Mercutio's energetic imagination explodes into life with his fantastic 'Queen Mab' speech.

The speech is sheer invention, and must be enjoyed as such—having no deeply significant meaning, and no particular relevance to the action of the play (except to allow enough time for Capulet's guests to eat their supper).

Before the masquers leave the stage Romeo voices his unease, and then resigns himself to fate.

SCENE 5    The stage is now filled with activity as the Capulet servants rush about, moving furniture and dishes, indicating that the meal is over and that the dancing is about to begin. Once again we are inside Capulet's house.

Capulet is a jovial host and welcomes the masquers in a happy mood, recalling the masquerades that he himself took part in when he was a young man. The masquers mix with the guests in the dance; two old men (Capulet and his cousin) chat about their acquaintances; and Romeo catches sight of Juliet.

Romeo is overwhelmed by Juliet's beauty. But whilst he stands in wonder he is observed by Tybalt, who recognizes him as an enemy. Tybalt's reaction is immediate: a foe means a fight. Fortunately Capulet is watching, and we see that the older man has become a little wiser since this morning. He restrains Tybalt—but we realize that his restraint will not be effective for very long.

The disagreement between Capulet and his nephew has given Romeo time to approach Juliet, and we must imagine the two lovers standing quite apart from the rest of the characters on stage. The dancing continues, but they are not a part of it. Their separateness is emphasized by the form of the verse in which they have begun to speak.

Romeo starts with devout religious utterance:

> If I profane with my unworthiest hand
> This holy shrine . . .

He develops the religious image for four lines which rhyme alternately (abab), then Juliet picks up the same image, speaking the next four lines in the same pattern (with rhyme cbcb). A third quatrain is shared between the two (rhyme dede) and a final couplet is spoken—the first line by Juliet, the second by Romeo, who clearly takes advantage to kiss Juliet at the end of his line.

> Then move not while my prayers' effect I take.

The fourteen lines are in fact a sonnet—a complex and highly artificial verse form, popular in the sixteenth century and generally regarded as the proper medium for love poetry. The form is used to emphasize the lovers' isolation from the society in which they live; and the way in which they share the same extended image and same verse form emphasizes the harmony of their thoughts. Even so, we must notice that Juliet manages to tease Romeo a little within the solemn expression of devotion. After the kiss, it appears that the lovers are about to start a second sonnet; but this is interrupted by the Nurse.

Now the lovers must be brought back from the state of isolation to the real world; and they must begin to understand what has happened to them. The Nurse chats to Romeo and answers his question in a very down-to-earth way: she explains that Juliet is the daughter of the host and that the man who 'can lay hold of her Shall have the chinks' (i.e. he will be rich). Then it is time for the masquerade to end.

And now Juliet must learn the truth. Once again the Nurse is the source of information. The last lines of the scene combine ordinary speech with formal rhymed couplets, and we can see that Juliet's mind is working on two levels of thought: her questions to the Nurse are naturalistic, but her inner thoughts—spoken for the hearing of the audience alone—are prophetic.

CHORUS    'The use of this Chorus is not easily discovered.' These are the words of one of the first and greatest of Shakespeare's editors, Dr Samuel Johnson, who was writing in the eighteenth century. He complained that the information given in the speech is unnecessary; and indeed it is! But look at the play from the point of view of an actor—the actor playing the part of Romeo. He has just had to switch from an intense love-duet to a sudden and deep foreboding as he realises his life is at risk. He leaves the stage in *Act 1*, Scene 5 at line 126; the scene ends less than twenty lines later, and *Act 2*, Scene 1 demands Romeo's appearance almost immediately. The fourteen lines (another sonnet) spoken by the Chorus are necessary to allow the actor to get his breath back, and perhaps even to dash round the back of the stage, and enter from the opposite side, so that the audience does not think he has returned to the ballroom.

## ACT 2

SCENE 1  We now have to pay close attention to the words of the actors when they mention the location of the scenes that follow. Benvolio tells us that Romeo, after speaking two lines, has disappeared and 'leapt this orchard wall'. Whilst Mercutio and Benvolio fool around on one side of the wall—outside the orchard—Romeo lurks on the other side, hearing Mercutio's jokes, but not responding.

Mercutio is in high spirits. He calls for his friend, pretending to be a magician who can raise the ghosts of the dead by calling on the name of a deity. He invokes Venus and Cupid, and then decides that Rosaline is the goddess whom Romeo worships—with sexual, not spiritual desire. Like the 'Queen Mab' speech, this display of verbal fireworks is delightful for itself; but it also presents two different aspects of love. We are reminded of Romeo's passion for Rosaline—the fanciful emotion that made him feel ill, yet which he indulged because (probably) he had nothing better to do, and where he worshipped Rosaline as a goddess. Mercutio's attitude to women is in complete contrast; there is no emotion at all here, only sexual desire. We shall now be shown a third kind of love—one which has elements of the other two, but which is far more powerful than either of them.

Mercutio and Benvolio decide that they might just as well go home to bed, since they cannot find Romeo:

'tis in vain
To seek him here that means not to be found.

SCENE 2  The verse does not allow any break in the action; Romeo completes the couplet:

He jests at scars that never felt a wound.

We must, however, be aware that the setting has changed: we are now *inside* the orchard, and Romeo is looking up at the light shining through a window.

He begins to speak about his love for Juliet. At first there seems to be very little difference between *this* love, and the emotion he pretended to feel for Rosaline:

> Arise, fair sun, and kill the envious moon,
> Who is already sick and pale with grief,
> That thou, her maid, art far more fair than she.

This is the conventional language of love poetry: it was fashionable for lovers to speak in this way on stage. Very quickly, however, the language becomes more simple as Romeo learns to express genuine feelings:

> It is my lady, O it is my love:
> O that she knew she were!

That second line is especially effective *because* it is incomplete—there are three poetic 'feet' instead of five; we have become accustomed to the rhythm of the pentameter, so we wait for the completion of the line, and the silence indicates that Romeo cannot find words to express his thoughts.

The Elizabethan stage had a small area (probably at the centre back) which had curtains, and a roof supported by pillars. Actors could come on to the main, open stage through the curtains; or they could appear and act short scenes on a balcony above, which supplied a second acting level. Now this becomes the balcony outside Juliet's bedroom; Juliet comes out into the night, believing that she is alone, and begins to speak of her love for Romeo.

Fear and delight are mingled in Juliet's heart. She has found a 'dear perfection' in Romeo's person, but she knows well that his name is her enemy—because 'Romeo' is one of the family names of the Montagues. Juliet is startled, even a little embarrassed, when she realizes that Romeo has overheard her private thoughts, but soon the two lovers are able to discuss their feelings with simple honesty. The mood of the scene varies between intense passion and gentle teasing. It is interrupted when the Nurse calls to Juliet from within—she is off-stage, and we must imagine her to be waiting in Juliet's bedroom. The effect is the same as that achieved in the ballroom scene, when the lovers were drawn back from the isolation of their love into the real world. After the interruption they renew their promises to each other. Suddenly Juliet makes a proposal which must come as a surprise (although a delightful one) to her new lover:

> If that thy bent of love be honourable,

> Thy purpose marriage, send me word tomorrow . . .
> Where and what time thou wilt perform the rite

Only a few moments before, Juliet had expressed her anxieties about this new relationship: 'It is too rash, too unadvis'd, too sudden'. Now she seems to have forgotten the worry, or else her love has become so strong that she cannot restrain herself.

When the lovers have finally separated, and Juliet has returned to her bedroom, Romeo is eager to act on his beloved's suggestion.

SCENE 3    It is Monday morning:

> The grey-ey'd morn smiles on the frowning night,
> Chequ'ring the eastern clouds with streaks of light.

The scene changes completely now, as we go ahead of Romeo to Friar Lawrence's 'close cell', where the holy man devotes his time to prayer, study, and the concoction of medicines from the herbs that grow around his home. He delivers a short lecture on herbal drugs that can kill and cure. Once again this allows Romeo to travel from one location—the Capulet orchard at daybreak—to another: the friar's cell, where he arrives 'ere the sun advance his burning eye'.

He confesses everything to Friar Lawrence. The friar is clearly accustomed to hearing Romeo's confessions of love and has obviously given him sound advice in the past (which Romeo has ignored until now). Friar Lawrence can see a way in which this new love between Romeo and Juliet—Montague and Capulet—could perhaps be turned to an even greater good. It might make peace between the two families: 'turn your households' rancour to pure love'.

SCENE 4    After the solemn interview with the friar, the mood and scene of the play change completely. Back in the city of Verona Romeo's two friends, Benvolio and Mercutio, are fresh and full of energy; presumably they have been able to sleep a little—and at least they have changed out of their masquerade costumes. Romeo, when he joins them at line 37, is still wearing fancy dress: Mercutio jokes about it—'Signor Romeo, "bon jour"! There's a French salutation to your French slop.'

Before Romeo appears, the two young men have been discussing Tybalt, the fierce nephew of Capulet who had tried to attack Romeo at the masquerade. Capulet's restraint has not lasted long: Tybalt has already, we hear, sent a letter to Romeo challenging him to fight a duel. Mercutio describes Tybalt, and his words reveal the same excited imagination that presented Queen Mab to us. Mercutio laughs at Tybalt and his affectations—his correct fencing technique, his accent, and his fondness for using the latest slang expressions. At the same time, however, he has some respect: Tybalt is not to be taken lightly—he is 'More than Prince of Cats'. This passage serves to remind us of the character whom we met for a short time at Capulet's party, and to prepare us for his second appearance.

Romeo joins his friends, and all three engage in witty chatter; they are full of energy, and the outlet for this energy is (at the moment) verbal fighting in the best of friendly relationships. At the height of the fun, Juliet's Nurse appears. She is apparently wearing some flowing dress and perhaps she is a rather large woman: as she comes into view Romeo pretends that she is a ship ('A sail, a sail!'). The Nurse— pretending to be shocked by the bawdy jokes but really enjoying them —delivers Juliet's message in her rambling prose. Since we already know what the message is, we can concentrate on the comedy of the Nurse's speech. The action of the play is now moving very fast; it is still Monday, and the time is twelve noon.

SCENE 5    For Juliet, however, the time seems to pass slowly. Her Nurse has been away since nine o'clock, 'and from nine till twelve Is three long hours'. More comedy follows when the Nurse returns with Romeo's greetings and instructions to his love: the Nurse is in a mischievous mood and enjoys keeping Juliet in suspense. She encourages the girl's expectations:

> Your love says, like an honest gentleman,
> And a courteous, and a kind, and a handsome . . .

She can see that Juliet grows more excited with every word—and so she breaks off, ceasing her praise of Romeo to ask a plain question on quite another matter: 'Where is your mother?' The great news—that the marriage ceremony has been arranged—is communicated simply, mixed with the Nurse's complaints about the trials that she must undergo to serve the child she loves. She sends Juliet to the wedding— and she herself goes for her dinner.

SCENE 6    At Friar Lawrence's cell, the bridegroom waits eagerly for his bride. The friar's words of hesitation and foreboding do not diminish Romeo's delight, and very soon he is rewarded by the appearance of Juliet. A few brief words of love are spoken by each of the two before the friar hurries them off to his chapel, refusing to let them 'stay alone Till Holy Church incorporate two in one.'

## ACT 3

SCENE 1

Italian summer afternoons are hot, and it is sensible to take a rest in the shade, or even indoors. Benvolio recommends this to Mercutio, pointing out that members of the Capulet family are about in the streets, 'And if we meet we shall not scape a brawl'. Mercutio responds with his usual good-natured humour, but his invention seems slower than usual; probably he too feels hot and rather tired. His energy is restored when Tybalt appears, in search of Romeo and determined to fight. Mercutio is outraged when Romeo receives Tybalt's abuse with mildness, and draws his own sword to attack the Capulet.

Romeo tries to stop the fighting; his interference seems to distract Mercutio, and he fails to dodge Tybalt's sword. We are shown the accuracy of Tybalt's fencing, described earlier by Mercutio: 'one, two, and the third in your bosom' (2, 4, 22). Even at the point of death, Mercutio is witty. His wit, as much as his curse on the houses of Montague and Capulet alike, awakens Romeo's own sense of honour. For a moment he forgets his new bride and takes his sword to attack her cousin in an act of vengeance for the death of Mercutio.

Once again the citizens of Verona rush to the scene of the fighting; and once again Prince Escales appears and tries to enforce peace. The first time that we saw this (*Act 1*, Scene 1) the intervention came before any harm was done. This time it is too late. Mercutio's body has been taken from the scene, but Tybalt lies at Romeo's feet, and the blood-stained sword is in Romeo's hand.

Prince Escales hears of the sequence of events from Benvolio's mouth, and he listens to the pleas of Lady Capulet and Montague, who speak as representatives of the warring families. Escales promises strict justice. His first ruling is to banish Romeo from Verona:

> Let Romeo hence in haste,
> Else, when he is found, that hour is his last.

Escales has no choice. Romeo has broken the law and must be duly punished; otherwise, all civil law will break down, and a state of anarchy will result:

> Mercy but murders, pardoning those that kill.

SCENE 2    Ignorant of what is happening in Verona's streets, Juliet longs for night to come, when Romeo will 'Leap to these arms untalk'd of and unseen'. She is passionately in love, with a physical longing to possess Romeo and to be possessed by him in an ecstasy of impatience. But the Nurse shatters her dreams with the confused reports of death and banishment, Tybalt and Romeo. Juliet's heart and mind are torn by conflicting emotions as she struggles to understand what the Nurse is saying. At the end of the scene she subsides into grief for the loss of her husband, and sends the Nurse to look for him at Friar Lawrence's cell.

SCENE 3    The Friar is trying to calm Romeo, preaching the virtue of stoic resignation to fate and pointing out that things might be worse. Romeo is condemned to banishment, not to death. But for Romeo, banishment from Verona means separation from Juliet, and this is worse than death. When the Nurse tells of Juliet's grief, Romeo's distress increases and he is ready to kill himself. The friar, however, has a plan; and after another lecture (which is much admired by the Nurse) he takes control of the situation.

SCENE 4    So much has happened in such a short time that the characters themselves find it difficult to remember what day it is. Capulet has to ask Paris, 'But soft, what day is this?' It is still only Monday. Juliet has gone to bed, and Capulet himself 'would have been abed an hour ago' had it not been for the presence of the County Paris, who wants to know whether or not he can marry Juliet.

   Capulet reaches a sudden decision: Paris shall marry his daughter, and the wedding will be held that same week, on Thursday. It will not be a grand occasion, because the family is in mourning for the death of Tybalt: there will be 'some half a dozen friends, And there an end.'

   It is time for bed; in fact 'it is so very late that we May call it early by and by'.

SCENE 5    For Romeo and Juliet it is far too early. Romeo has obeyed the friar, climbed the balcony to Juliet's bedroom, and consummated the marriage whose religious ceremony was performed on Monday afternoon. Without the physical consummation, the marriage would not have been complete; the vows would not be irrevocable—Romeo and Juliet would not have been man and wife.

   Now they must be separated. The birdsong they hear comes from the lark, the first bird to sing in the morning, and the light in the east heralds the rising sun. Romeo must save his life by escaping to Mantua.

The lovers' farewells are interrupted by the Nurse, warning that Lady Capulet is looking for her daughter. Romeo climbs down from the balcony and Juliet, standing above, imagines that she sees him, 'As one dead in the bottom of a tomb'.

Lady Capulet probably enters on to the main stage below Juliet's balcony; the restricted space of the upper acting-level would not be able to accommodate all the members of the Capulet family (including the Nurse) who are needed for the rest of the scene.

Juliet's mother is cold and unsympathetic. She does not understand her daughter's grief, of course, and naturally assumes that the tears are for Tybalt. Juliet's words deceive Lady Capulet, but their meaning is clear to the audience when she speaks of her anguish and her longing to be close to the man who murdered her cousin. She speaks politely to her mother, addressing her formally as 'Madam' and 'your ladyship', and appearing to be thankful for the promised 'day of joy' that is so unexpected. But when she learns of the nature of the celebration, Juliet forgets all her obedience and good manners. The news is a shock; obstinate refusal to marry Paris is the only possible reaction.

Juliet's father enters. His own distress at the death of his nephew turns to sympathy with what he believes to be Juliet's grief for Tybalt. But sorrow instantly turns to rage when he learns that Juliet has refused the offered marriage. He bullies and threatens, cursing his daughter and swearing at the Nurse. In a storm of anger he leaves the stage, followed by his wife, who, like him, has disowned their child: 'Do as thou wilt, for I have done with thee'.

Juliet demands comfort from her Nurse, whom she has loved and trusted for fourteen years. But the Nurse has no comfort to offer. She too has experienced grief and shock at the events of the previous day, and now she can only think of the most practical way of getting out of all their difficulties. No one knows about the marriage to Romeo; he is now banished and will never dare to return to Verona and claim Juliet as his wife. It would be so easy if Juliet were to forget about Romeo, and marry Paris—who, after all, is 'a lovely gentleman'.

Juliet is completely alone.

## Act 4

SCENE 1   Whilst the Capulet household is in an uproar of conflicting passions, the County Paris has acted quickly and efficiently. We find him with Friar Lawrence, making arrangements for the wedding. He speaks gentle and affectionate words to Juliet when she appears, and Juliet replies with calm courtesy. When she is alone with the friar, however, Juliet gives way to her grief once more, threatening to kill herself rather than break the sacred vow she made to Romeo. Her passion becomes hysterical as she describes what she will suffer rather than marry Paris:

> chain me with roaring bears,
> Or hide me nightly in a charnel-house,
> O'ercover'd quite with dead men's rattling bones . . .

Friar Lawrence can offer a solution—although even this is not free from fear and danger. His researches into the medicinal qualities of herbs have allowed him to concoct a 'distilling liquor' which Juliet must drink. She will fall into a coma; everyone will believe she is dead. She will be laid in the family vault, and there she will sleep until Romeo, recalled from Mantua by Friar Lawrence, comes to rescue her.

SCENE 2  The conference with Friar Lawrence is reassuring, and when Juliet returns home she is able to ask her father's forgiveness. We find Capulet in a state of excitement, preparing for the wedding: he seems to have forgotten that he had decided to invite only 'some half a dozen friends' (3, 4, 27)—now he is asking for 'twenty cunning cooks'. Pleased with Juliet's new obedience, he decides to have the wedding one day early: 'We'll to church tomorrow'.

This is still Tuesday, but it is quite late: Lady Capulet points out that it is 'now near night' when she attempts to change her husband's mind, but Capulet is firm; he will take care of the preparations:

> I'll not to bed tonight; let me alone,
> I'll play the huswife for this once.

SCENE 3  Juliet and her Nurse have also been preparing for the wedding, choosing Juliet's best clothes and jewels. Now Juliet asks to be left alone. She is excited and frightened—perhaps the friar's drug is really a poison; perhaps she will wake up to find herself alone in the vault among the dead bodies . . . She is terrified; but she drinks the potion.

SCENE 4  Very early in the morning—Capulet points out that ''tis three a'clock'—the servants are rushing around making preparations for the feast. The Nurse is sent to wake Juliet. The bridegroom, the County Paris, has arrived to claim his bride. He has brought musicians with him, to wake Juliet and accompany the happy couple throughout the day. This has become quite a grand wedding, in the English style of the sixteenth century.

SCENE 5    The curtains are drawn around Juliet's bed, and the Nurse chatters to her mistress, whom she is unable to see. The discovery is slow: the Nurse sees that Juliet is sleeping; then that she is fully dressed; finally, that she appears to be dead. Lady Capulet is called to the scene, then Juliet's father, and then Paris and Friar Lawrence. A general lamentation follows, and each of the characters is allowed a short recitation of grief.

The scene is not an easy one to act. The audience cannot share the emotions expressed by the characters, because we know the truth: Juliet is not dead, and all this is unnecessary. We must save our tears—we shall need them later. To prevent undue audience involvement, Shakespeare gives the characters an exaggerated kind of verse; there are too many words, and they are too strong for us to pay much attention to their meaning. All four recitations start with a list of adjectives, and the effect is *almost* comic—we find it difficult to sympathize with the father who expresses himself in this way:

> Despis'd, distressed, hated, martyr'd, kill'd!
> Uncomfortable time, why cam'st thou now
> To murder, murder our solemnity?

Friar Lawrence preaches a short funeral sermon and gives instructions for the removal of Juliet's body.

The musicians try to comprehend what is happening. They are not deeply involved, but they will wait for the mourners, and accompany them to the churchyard.

## ACT 5

SCENE 1    Bad news travels fast, and that same day (Wednesday) Romeo is informed of the catastrophe that has befallen his bride and her family. He is safe in Mantua, but life has no meaning for him now. He describes an apothecary's shop, whose owner is so poor that he can be bribed to sell poison. The sale is completed, and Romeo leaves for Verona.

SCENE 2    But Romeo was given the wrong information. We hear now how Friar John, who should have delivered a letter to Romeo, was prevented from leaving Verona. In this scene we cannot fail to realize that Shakespeare's time-scheme for *Romeo and Juliet* is too compressed; perhaps the dramatist was himself working at high speed when he condensed the nine months of Arthur Brooke's narrative action into a mere five days.

The short scene, however, allows Romeo to travel from Mantua to Verona, arriving outside the Capulet vault on Wednesday night.

SCENE 3 Juliet's tomb already has a visitor—the County Paris, who has vowed to bring flowers and scented water to the grave every night. His ritual is interrupted by the arrival of Romeo, who proceeds to force open the tomb where he expects to find his wife's body.

Romeo is no longer the dreamy youth that we met at the beginning of the play. He describes himself as 'a desperate man' and, when Paris ignores his gentle warning, he fights with a serious determination which is totally different from the rough assaults of the servants (*Act 1*, Scene 1) and from the elegant sword-play of the young noblemen (*Act 3*, Scene 1). Romeo intends to kill Paris without ceremony and without delay.

He has no regrets when he has killed Paris, but he feels pity for the 'Good gentle youth'. He is preparing to lay Paris, tenderly, in the tomb when he looks on Juliet's face. Although he is prepared for death, he in fact sees life: 'beauty's ensign yet Is crimson in thy lips and in thy cheeks'. The audience knows that he is not deceived, and the tension is great. Juliet *might* wake in time; all might yet be well.

The hope is in vain, of course. Romeo drinks his poison, whose action is swift: he dies kissing Juliet, a second before Friar Lawrence, stumbling in the graveyard, enters the tomb to comfort Juliet in her waking moments. Juliet seems refreshed after her sleep, but her resolution is not diminished. As soon as she understands the situation, she acts—first kissing the poison on Romeo's lips, then making sure of her death with Romeo's dagger, which she plunges into her own breast: 'O happy dagger, This is thy sheath'.

Once again the citizens of Verona are drawn to the scene, and Prince Escales appears among them. Friar Lawrence provides the narrative this time, freely confessing his own part in the events and offering himself for punishment. The County's Page and Balthasar fill in some missing details. Capulet and Montague join hands; they have paid a high price for their new friendship, and there is not much to be said:

> A glooming peace this morning with it brings,
> The sun for sorrow will not show his head.

It is Thursday morning.

# Shakespeare's Verse

Easily the best way to understand and appreciate Shakespeare's verse is to read it aloud—and don't worry if you don't understand everything! Try not to be too influenced by the dominant rhythm. Instead decide which are the most important words in each line and use the regular metre to drive them forward to the listeners.

### Blank verse

Shakespeare's plays are written mainly in 'blank verse', the form preferred by most dramatists in the sixteenth and early seventeenth centuries. Blank verse has a regular rhythm, but does not rhyme. It is a very flexible medium which is capable – like the human speaking voice – of a wide range of tones. Shakespeare used a particular form of blank verse called iambic pentameter.

### Iambic pentameter

In iambic pentameter the lines are ten syllables long. Each line is divided into pairs of syllables, or 'feet'. Each 'foot' has one stressed and one unstressed syllable—a patern which often appears in normal English speech. Here is an example:

> **Tybalt**
> What, árt thou dráwn amóng these héartless hínds?
> Túrn thee, Benvólio, loók upón thy déath.
> **Benvolio**
> I dó but keép the péace. Put úp thy swórd,
> Or mánage ít to párt these mén with mé.
> **Tybalt**
> What, dráwn, and tálk of péace? I háte the wórd,
> As Í hate héll, all Móntagúes, and theé.
> Have át thee, cóward.                                    *1, 1, 60–6*

Here the pentameter accommodates a variety of speech tones—Tybalt's angry challenge, Benvolio's steady calm, and the scorn and hatred with which Tybalt renews his attack.

### Varying stresses

In the quotation above, most of the lines are regular in length and follow the normal iambic stress pattern. But sometimes Shakespeare deviates from the norm, varying the stress patterns for unusual emphasis, and writing lines that are longer or shorter than ten syllables. The stress is reversed, for instance, in Tybalt's 'Turn thee', and a threatening movement (rather than words) completes the line after 'coward'.

### Dividing ideas

The speech of Prince Escales, a little later in this scene, demonstrates another feature of Shakespeare's verse.

> **Prince**
> On páin of tórture, fróm those blóody hánds
> Throw yóur mistémper'd wéapons tó the gróund,
> And héar the séntence óf your móved prince.

*1, 1, 80–2*

This example shows how sometimes the grammatical unit of meaning is contained within the verse line:

> And hear the sentence of your moved prince.

This allows for a pause at the end of the line, before a new idea is started. At other times, the sense runs on from one line to the next:

> from those bloody hands
> Throw your mistemper'd weapons to the ground.

This allows for the natural fluidity of speech, avoiding monotony but still maintaining the iambic rhythm.

## Source, Text, and Date

For the source of his play Shakespeare relies almost entirely on a narrative poem, *The Tragicall History of Romeus and Juliet* by Arthur Brooke, which was published in 1562 and is itself a translation of a popular prose fiction by Bandello (published 1554)—which in turn derives from even earlier Italian stories.

*Romeo and Juliet* was probably written between 1594 and 1596, and it was first published in a quarto edition of 1597 (Q1). The quality of the text printed here suggests that this is a pirated edition, lacking the authority of either the dramatist or the acting company that performed the play. It might have been printed from a manuscript that one or two of the actors, knowing its popularity, had constructed from memory and sold to some unscrupulous printers. Although the actors' memories were often faulty, and many speeches were mis-recollected, garbled, or even forgotten altogether, the edition is helpful for its stage directions and their suggestions of early theatre practice.

Another version of the play (Q2) was published in 1599, and the titlepage of this quarto—which is the basis of all modern editions—claimed that the text was 'Newly corrected, augmented, and amended'. Shakespeare's own manuscript was probably available to the printer of Q2, although occasionally—perhaps where the handwriting was illegible—he turned to the printed text of Q1.

The present edition is based on the text established by G. Blakemore Evans in 1984 for the New Cambridge Shakespeare.

# Romeo & Juliet

# Characters in the Play

| | |
|---|---|
| Escales | *Prince of Verona* |
| Mercutio | *his kinsman, Romeo's friend* |
| The County Paris | *another kinsman, suitor to* Juliet |
| | *('County' = Count)* |
| | |
| Montague | *head of a noble family in Verona which has been at enmity with the* Capulets *for a long time* |
| Lady Montague | *his wife* |
| Romeo | *his son* |
| Benvolio | *his nephew, Romeo's friend* |
| Abram ⎫<br>Balthasar ⎭ | *servants of* Montague |
| | |
| Capulet | *head of a noble family in Verona which is hostile to the* Montagues |
| Lady Capulet | *his wife* |
| Juliet | *his daughter* |
| Cousin Capulet | *his relative* |
| Tybalt | Lady Capulet's *nephew* |
| Nurse | *to* Juliet |
| | |
| Peter ⎫<br>Sampson ⎬<br>Gregory ⎭ | *servants of* Capulet |
| | |
| Friar Lawrence ⎫<br>Friar John ⎭ | *Franciscan friars* |
| An Apothecary | |
| Three Musicians | |
| The Chorus | |

Citizens of Verona, masquers, pages, servants, watchmen

Except for *Act 5*, Scene 1, the action of the play takes place in Verona

# THE PROLOGUE

**The Prologue**

0s.d. *Chorus*: In early English drama the Chorus, played by a single actor, was used to explain and comment on the action.

1 *households*: families.
 *dignity*: nobility.

2 *lay*: set.

3 *grudge*: quarrel.
 *mutiny*: violence.

4 *civil*: belonging to fellow-citizens.

5 *From forth*: bred from.

6 *star-cross'd*: ill-fated.

7 *misadventur'd*: unfortunate.
 *overthrows*: disasters.

8 *Doth*: do; an old plural form still sometimes found in Elizabethan English.

9 *passage*: course.
 *death-mark'd*: doomed to death.

11 *but . . . end*: only the deaths of their children.
 *remove*: stop.

12 *two hours' traffic*: business lasting for two hours.

14 *What . . . miss*: what is omitted in this Prologue (which, in form, is a perfect sonnet).

*Enter* Chorus

Two households, both alike in dignity,
In fair Verona (where we lay our scene),
From ancient grudge break to new mutiny,
Where civil blood makes civil hands unclean.
5 From forth the fatal loins of these two foes
A pair of star-cross'd lovers take their life;
Whose misadventur'd piteous overthrows
Doth with their death bury their parents' strife.
The fearful passage of their death-mark'd love,
10 And the continuance of their parents' rage,
Which but their children's end nought could remove,
Is now the two hours' traffic of our stage;
The which if you with patient ears attend,
What here shall miss, our toil shall strive to mend.

[*Exit*

# ACT 1

**Act 1 Scene 1**

Fighting breaks out between Capulets and Montagues and the Prince must intervene to stop them. Romeo's parents are worried about his strange behaviour, but Romeo explains to his friend Benvolio that he is in love with Rosaline.

Os.d. *with . . . Capulet*: Servants, who carried heavy swords and small shields ('bucklers'), wore badges to identify their masters.

1 *carry coals*: be insulted (a current slang expression).

2 *colliers*: men who deal in coal (proverbially said to be dirty and dishonest).

3 *and*: if.
*choler*: anger; Sampson makes a pun—which Gregory continues.
*draw*: draw our swords.

4 *while you live*: whatever you do.
*draw . . . collar*: avoid the hangman's noose.

5 *moved*: aroused; Sampson seems to invite Gregory's misinterpretation.

6 *not . . . strike*: you are not easily so aroused that you will fight.

7 *a dog . . . Montague*: any of that Montague lot (a contemptuous reference).

8 *stand*: stand firm (and fight).

10–11 *take the wall of*: show myself better than; in Elizabethan streets it was cleaner and safer to walk near the wall.

12–13 *the weakest . . . wall*: A proverbial saying meaning 'the weakest yields in a struggle'.

14 *the weaker vessels*: A biblical expression deriving from 1 Peter 3:7: 'husbands . . . giv[ing] honour unto the woman, as unto the weaker vessel'.

15 *thrust to the wall*: pushed against the wall (in sexual encounters).

18 *men*: servants; Gregory may also mean that they have no quarrel with the women.

## SCENE 1

*Sunday morning: a public place. Enter* Sampson *and* Gregory, *with swords and bucklers, of the house of Capulet*

**Sampson**
Gregory, on my word, we'll not carry coals.
**Gregory**
No, for then we should be colliers.
**Sampson**
I mean, and we be in choler, we'll draw.
**Gregory**
Ay, while you live, draw your neck out of collar.
**Sampson**
5 I strike quickly, being moved.
**Gregory**
But thou art not quickly moved to strike.
**Sampson**
A dog of the house of Montague moves me.
**Gregory**
To move is to stir, and to be valiant is to stand: therefore if thou art moved thou runn'st away.
**Sampson**
10 A dog of that house shall move me to stand: I will take the wall of any man or maid of Montague's.
**Gregory**
That shows thee a weak slave, for the weakest goes to the wall.
**Sampson**
'Tis true, and therefore women being the weaker vessels
15 are ever thrust to the wall: therefore I will push Montague's men from the wall, and thrust his maids to the wall.
**Gregory**
The quarrel is between our masters, and us their men.

19  *'Tis all one*: it makes no difference.

20  *civil*: friendly; Sampson perhaps thinks this is proper conduct for a tyrant.

23  *maidenheads*: virginities.

24  *in what sense*: with whatever meaning.

25  *in sense*: in sensation, in feeling.

26  *stand*: keep erect.

27  *a pretty . . . flesh*: a fine figure of a man, sexually well endowed.

29  *poor-John*: dried salted hake (Gregory insults Sampson's virility).
    *tool*: weapon.

29–30  *of . . . Montagues*: some of Montague's men.

31  *back*: support.

34  *marry*: by the Virgin Mary (a mild oath).

35  *take . . . sides*: keep within the law.

36  *list*: like.

37  *bite my thumb*: make a gesture of defiance (by jerking the thumb nail forward from the front teeth).

**Sampson**
'Tis all one, I will show myself a tyrant: when I have

20  fought with the men, I will be civil with the maids; I will cut off their heads.

**Gregory**
The heads of the maids?

**Sampson**
Ay, the heads of the maids, or their maidenheads, take it in what sense thou wilt.

**Gregory**

25  They must take it in sense that feel it.

**Sampson**
Me they shall feel while I am able to stand, and 'tis known I am a pretty piece of flesh.

**Gregory**
'Tis well thou art not fish; if thou hadst, thou hadst been poor-John. Draw thy tool, here comes of the house of

30  Montagues.

*Enter two* Servingmen, Abram *and* Balthasar

**Sampson**
My naked weapon is out. Quarrel, I will back thee.

**Gregory**
How, turn thy back and run?

**Sampson**
Fear me not.

**Gregory**
No, marry, I fear thee!

**Sampson**

35  Let us take the law of our sides, let them begin.

**Gregory**
I will frown as I pass by, and let them take it as they list.

**Sampson**
Nay, as they dare. I will bite my thumb at them, which is disgrace to them if they bear it.

**Abram**
Do you bite your thumb at us, sir?

**Sampson**

40  I do bite my thumb, sir.

**Abram**
Do you bite your thumb at us, sir?

**Sampson**
[*Aside to* Gregory] Is the law of our side if I say ay?

**Gregory**
[*Aside to* Sampson] No.

**Sampson**
No, sir, I do not bite my thumb at you, sir, but I bite my
45 thumb, sir.

**Gregory**
Do you quarrel, sir?

**Abram**
Quarrel, sir? No, sir.

**Sampson**
But if you do, sir, I am for you. I serve as good a man as
you.

**Abram**
50 No better.

**Sampson**
Well, sir.

*Enter* Benvolio

**Gregory**
[*Aside to* Sampson] Say 'better', here comes one of my
master's kinsmen.

**Sampson**
Yes, better, sir.

**Abram**
55 You lie.

**Sampson**
Draw, if you be men. Gregory, remember thy washing
blow.

*They fight*

**Benvolio**
Part, fools!
Put up your swords, you know not what you do.

*Beats down their swords*

48 *I am for you*: I will join the quarrel with you.

56 *washing*: slashing with great force.

59 *Put up*: sheathe.

*Enter* Tybalt

**Tybalt**
60  What, art thou drawn among these heartless hinds?
Turn thee, Benvolio, look upon thy death.
**Benvolio**
I do but keep the peace. Put up thy sword,
Or manage it to part these men with me.
**Tybalt**
What, drawn and talk of peace? I hate the word,
65  As I hate hell, all Montagues, and thee.
Have at thee, coward.

*They fight*

*Enter several of both houses, who join the fray, and
three or four* Citizens *as* Officers *of the Watch, with
clubs or partisans*

**Officers**
Clubs, bills, and partisans! Strike! Beat them down!
Down with the Capulets! Down with the Montagues!

*Enter old* Capulet *in his gown, and his wife* Lady
Capulet

**Capulet**
What noise is this? Give me my long sword, ho!
**Lady Capulet**
70  A crutch, a crutch! why call you for a sword?
**Capulet**
My sword, I say! old Montague is come,
And flourishes his blade in spite of me.

*Enter old* Montague *and his wife* Lady Montague

**Montague**
Thou villain Capulet!—Hold me not, let me go.
**Lady Montague**
Thou shalt not stir one foot to seek a foe.

60  *art thou drawn*: is your sword drawn.
*heartless hinds*: (a) servants who lack
courage ('heart'); (b) female deer
without a male leader ('hart').
62  *but*: only.
63  *manage it*: use it properly.
*part*: separate.

66  *Have at thee*: Tybalt warns Benvolio
that he is about to attack.

67  *bills*: weapons with long handles and
axe-heads.
*partisans*: long staves with axe-heads.

68s.d.  *gown*: dressing-gown; the brawl
has disturbed the domestic peace of
the Capulet home.

69  *long sword*: an old-fashioned, heavy
weapon.

72  *spite*: defiance, scorn.

*Enter* Prince Escales *with his train*

**Prince**

75 Rebellious subjects, enemies to peace,
Profaners of this neighbour-stained steel—
Will they not hear?—What ho, you men, you beasts!
That quench the fire of your pernicious rage
With purple fountains issuing from your veins:
80 On pain of torture, from those bloody hands
Throw your mistemper'd weapons to the ground,
And hear the sentence of your moved prince.
Three civil brawls, bred of an airy word,
By thee, old Capulet, and Montague,
85 Have thrice disturb'd the quiet of our streets,
And made Verona's ancient citizens
Cast by their grave beseeming ornaments
To wield old partisans, in hands as old,
Canker'd with peace, to part your canker'd hate;
90 If ever you disturb our streets again,
Your lives shall pay the forfeit of the peace.
For this time all the rest depart away:
You, Capulet, shall go along with me,
And, Montague, come you this afternoon,
95 To know our farther pleasure in this case,
To old Free-town, our common judgement-place.
Once more, on pain of death, all men depart.
             [*Exeunt all but* Montague, Lady Montague, *and*
                                                    Benvolio

**Montague**

Who set this ancient quarrel new abroach?
Speak, nephew, were you by when it began?
**Benvolio**
100 Here were the servants of your adversary,
And yours, close fighting ere I did approach:
I drew to part them; in the instant came
The fiery Tybalt, with his sword prepar'd,
Which, as he breath'd defiance to my ears,
105 He swung about his head and cut the winds,
Who, nothing hurt withal, hiss'd him in scorn;
While we were interchanging thrusts and blows,
Came more and more, and fought on part and part,

---

76 *Profaners*: abusers, unworthy users.
*neighbour-stained steel*: stainèd;
weapons stained with the blood of
neighbours.

80 *On pain of torture*: with a penalty of
torture (for disobedience).
81 *mistemper'd*: (a) angry;
(b) intemperate, improper; (c) badly
made (steel is 'tempered' by being
hardened so that it becomes tough
and resilient).
82 *moved*: movèd; angry.
83 *bred . . . word*: caused by some trivial
remark.
87 *grave-beseeming ornaments*:
appropriately sober accessories.
88 *as old*: i.e. as old as the weapons.
89 *canker'd with peace*: rusty (because
unused in peacetime).
*canker'd hate*: malignant hatred.
91 *Your . . . peace*: you will be
condemned to death if you violate this
peace.

95 *know*: learn.
*our farther pleasure*: what else I
decide to do.
96 *common*: public.

98 *set . . . abroach*: opened up this old
quarrel; the phrase is used to describe
the opening of a cask of liquor or
gunpowder.
99 *by*: present.
101 *close fighting*: fighting hand to hand.
102 *drew*: drew my sword.
*in the instant*: at that moment.
103 *prepar'd*: already drawn.

106 *nothing hurt withal*: not injured by
Tybalt's flourishes.
108 *on part and part*: some on one side,
some on the other.

109 *parted either part*: separated both
    sides.

111 *Right*: very.
    *fray*: scuffle.
113 *Peer'd forth*: looked out from.
114 *drive*: drove.
115 *sycamore*: A tree sometimes
    associated with love-sickness (making
    a pun '*sickamour*').
116 *westward . . . side*: grows on the west
    side of this city.
118 *made*: went.
    *ware*: aware.
119 *covert*: concealment.
120 *measuring*: judging.
    *affections*: desires.
121 *most . . . found*: looked most for
    somewhere where I was least likely to
    be found.
122 *Being . . . self*: finding my own
    company too much for me.
123 *Pursu'd my humour*: followed my own
    inclinations.
    *not pursuing his*: not trying to
    understand Romeo's mood.
124 *gladly . . . from me*: was glad to avoid
    someone who was glad to escape from
    me.
126 *augmenting*: adding to.
128 *all so soon as*: just as soon as.
130 *curtains*: The best four-poster
    Elizabethan beds could be closed in
    with curtains.
    *Aurora*: the goddess of the dawn (in
    Greek mythology).
131 *my heavy son*: my sad son (Montague
    puns on 'sun' and 'light').
132 *pens*: shuts up.

Till the prince came, who parted either part.
 **Lady Montague**
110 O where is Romeo? saw you him today?
Right glad I am he was not at this fray.
 **Benvolio**
Madam, an hour before the worshipp'd sun
Peer'd forth the golden window of the east,
A troubled mind drive me to walk abroad,
115 Where underneath the grove of sycamore,
That westward rooteth from this city side,
So early walking did I see your son;
Towards him I made, but he was ware of me,
And stole into the covert of the wood;
120 I, measuring his affections by my own,
Which then most sought where most might not be
 found,
Being one too many by my weary self,
Pursu'd my humour, not pursuing his,
And gladly shunn'd who gladly fled from me.
 **Montague**
125 Many a morning hath he there been seen,
With tears augmenting the fresh morning's dew,
Adding to clouds more clouds with his deep sighs,
But all so soon as the all-cheering sun
Should in the farthest east begin to draw
130 The shady curtains from Aurora's bed,
Away from light steals home my heavy son,
And private in his chamber pens himself,
Shuts up his windows, locks fair daylight out,
And makes himself an artificial night:

135 *Black . . . prove*: Romeo's father is afraid that his son's depression may turn into melancholy, a clinical condition thought to arise from an excess of black bile.
*portentous*: ominous.
*humour*: mood.
138 *of*: from.

139 *importun'd . . . means*: questioned him in any way.

141 *his . . . counsellor*: acting as his own counsellor for his feelings.
142 *true*: wise (i.e. in the counsel he gives himself).
143 *close*: mysterious.
144 *sounding*: investigation (especially of water depths).
*discovery*: exploration.
145 *envious*: malicious.

149 *We . . . know*: I would be delighted to put it right when I know what it is.

150 *So please you*: if you please.
151 *his grievance*: what is worrying (grieving) him.
*or be much denied*: unless he is very firm in refusing to answer my questions.
152 *I . . . happy*: I hope you will be so lucky.
*by thy stay*: by staying here.
153 *true shrift*: confession of the truth.
154 *morrow*: morning.
*so young*: i.e. no later; Romeo was up very early in the morning.

135 Black and portentous must this humour prove,
Unless good counsel may the cause remove.
   **Benvolio**
My noble uncle, do you know the cause?
   **Montague**
I neither know it, nor can learn of him.
   **Benvolio**
Have you importun'd him by any means?
   **Montague**
140 Both by myself and many other friends,
But he, his own affections' counsellor,
Is to himself (I will not say how true)
But to himself so secret and so close,
So far from sounding and discovery,
145 As is the bud bit with an envious worm
Ere he can spread his sweet leaves to the air,
Or dedicate his beauty to the sun.
Could we but learn from whence his sorrows grow,
We would as willingly give cure as know.

*Enter* Romeo

   **Benvolio**
150 See where he comes. So please you step aside,
I'll know his grievance or be much denied.
   **Montague**
I would thou wert so happy by thy stay
To hear true shrift. Come, madam, let's away.
        [*Exeunt* Montague *and* Lady Montague
   **Benvolio**
Good morrow, cousin.
   **Romeo**
                Is the day so young?
   **Benvolio**
155 But new struck nine.
   **Romeo**
             Ay me, sad hours seem long.
Was that my father that went hence so fast?
   **Benvolio**
It was. What sadness lengthens Romeo's hours?

**Romeo**
Not having that, which, having, makes them short.
**Benvolio**
In love?
**Romeo**
160 Out—
**Benvolio**
Of love?
**Romeo**
Out of her favour where I am in love.
**Benvolio**
Alas that Love, so gentle in his view,
Should be so tyrannous and rough in proof!
**Romeo**
165 Alas that Love, whose view is muffled still,
Should, without eyes, see pathways to his will!
Where shall we dine? O me! what fray was here?
Yet tell me not, for I have heard it all:
Here's much to do with hate, but more with love:
170 Why then, O brawling love, O loving hate,
O any thing of nothing first create!
O heavy lightness, serious vanity,
Misshapen chaos of well-seeming forms,
Feather of lead, bright smoke, cold fire, sick health,
175 Still-waking sleep, that is not what it is!
This love feel I, that feel no love in this.
Dost thou not laugh?
**Benvolio**
                    No, coz, I rather weep.
**Romeo**
Good heart, at what?
**Benvolio**
                    At thy good heart's oppression.
**Romeo**
Why, such is love's transgression:
180 Griefs of mine own lie heavy in my breast,
Which thou wilt propagate to have it press'd
With more of thine; this love that thou hast shown
Doth add more grief to too much of mine own.
Love is a smoke made with the fume of sighs,

163 *in his view*: at first sight.

164 *in proof*: in fact, in experience.

165 *muffled still*: always obscured; the god of love is traditionally represented as a winged and blindfolded boy shooting arrows that cause humans to fall in love.

166 *Should . . . will*: should be able to do as he likes even though he can't see.
169 *much to do*: a great disturbance.
    *with hate*: i.e. with the feud between Montagues and Capulets.
    *with love*: i.e. the love of Romeo (a Montague) for Rosaline (a Capulet).
170 *brawling*: quarrelling.
171 *of nothing first create*: created out of nothing in the first place.
172 *serious vanity*: weighty emptiness.
173 *well-seeming*: apparently beautiful.
175 *Still-waking*: always awake.
176 *that . . . this*: have no love in return.
177 *coz*: cousin.
178 *oppression*: heavy burden.
179 *love's transgression*: the way love oversteps its proper limits.
181 *propagate*: increase; weights placed on the branches of trailing plants encourage new growth.
    *it*: Romeo's heart.

185 *purg'd*: purified.

187 *discreet*: discerning, discriminating.
188 *gall*: poison.
     *preserving*: healing.

189 *Soft*: wait a moment.
     *go along*: go with you.
190 *And if*: if.

192 *some other where*: somewhere else.

193 *in sadness*: seriously—but Romeo
     pretends to understand 'unhappily'.

199 *I aim'd so near*: I was nearly right.
     *suppos'd*: guessed.

200 *right good mark-man*: very good shot.
     *she's fair I love*: the woman I love is
     beautiful.
201 *a right fair mark*: a very clear
     mark( = target).
203 *Cupid's arrow*: see note to line 165.
     *Dian*: Diana, goddess of chastity in
     classical mythology.
     *wit*: sense, intelligence.
204 *proof*: armour.
205 *uncharm'd*: secure.
206 *will . . . terms*: will not be besieged by
     a lover's poetic language ('terms').
208 *ope . . . gold*: be tempted by gold that
     would seduce a saint; Romeo alludes
     to the myth of Danae who, though
     locked in a tower of bronze, was
     ravished by Zeus in a shower of gold.
209–10 *only . . . store*: she is poor only
     that when she dies, her fertility
     ('store') perishes with her beauty.
211 *still*: always.

185 Being purg'd, a fire sparkling in lovers' eyes,
    Being vex'd, a sea nourish'd with loving tears.
    What is it else? a madness most discreet,
    A choking gall, and a preserving sweet.
    Farewell, my coz.
        **Benvolio**
                      Soft, I will go along;
190 And if you leave me so, you do me wrong.
        **Romeo**
    Tut, I have lost myself, I am not here,
    This is not Romeo, he's some other where.
        **Benvolio**
    Tell me in sadness, who is that you love?
        **Romeo**
    What, shall I groan and tell thee?
        **Benvolio**
                              Groan? why, no;
195 But sadly tell me, who?
        **Romeo**
    Bid a sick man in sadness make his will—
    A word ill urg'd to one that is so ill:
    In sadness, cousin, I do love a woman.
        **Benvolio**
    I aim'd so near, when I suppos'd you lov'd.
        **Romeo**
200 A right good mark-man! and she's fair I love.
        **Benvolio**
    A right fair mark, fair coz, is soonest hit.
        **Romeo**
    Well, in that hit you miss: she'll not be hit
    With Cupid's arrow, she hath Dian's wit;
    And in strong proof of chastity well arm'd,
205 From Love's weak childish bow she lives uncharm'd.
    She will not stay the siege of loving terms,
    Nor bide th'encounter of assailing eyes,
    Nor ope her lap to saint-seducing gold.
    O, she is rich in beauty, only poor
210 That when she dies, with beauty dies her store.
        **Benvolio**
    Then she hath sworn that she will still live chaste?

212 *sparing*: economy.

213 *starv'd*: killed.

214 *Cuts . . . posterity*: denies her beauty to generations still to come.

215 *fair*: (a) lovely; (b) honest.

216 *To merit . . . despair*: earn heavenly happiness by condemning me to hell (the punishment for 'despair').

217 *forsworn to love*: sworn never to fall in love.

218 *live dead*: live as if I were dead.

222 *Examine . . . beauties*: look at other beautiful women.

223 *To call . . . more*: to make her beauty seem even more exquisite by comparison with others.

224 *happy*: lucky.

228 *passing fair*: surpassingly beautiful.

229 *note*: explanatory note.

230 *pass'd*: surpassed, excelled.

232 *I'll . . . doctrine*: I'll make you quite sure that my teaching ('doctrine') is right.
*die in debt*: die in the attempt.

**Romeo**

She hath, and in that sparing makes huge waste;
For beauty starv'd with her severity
Cuts beauty off from all posterity.
215 She is too fair, too wise, wisely too fair,
To merit bliss by making me despair.
She hath forsworn to love, and in that vow
Do I live dead, that live to tell it now.
    **Benvolio**
Be rul'd by me, forget to think of her.
    **Romeo**
220 O teach me how I should forget to think.
    **Benvolio**
By giving liberty unto thine eyes,
Examine other beauties.
    **Romeo**
                'Tis the way
To call hers (exquisite) in question more:
These happy masks that kiss fair ladies' brows,
225 Being black, puts us in mind they hide the fair;
He that is strucken blind cannot forget
The precious treasure of his eyesight lost;
Show me a mistress that is passing fair,
What doth her beauty serve but as a note
230 Where I may read who pass'd that passing fair?
Farewell, thou canst not teach me to forget.
    **Benvolio**
I'll pay that doctrine, or else die in debt.    [*Exeunt*

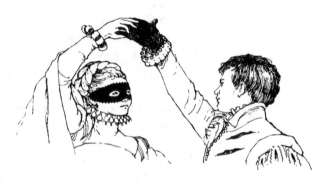

**Act 1 Scene 2**

Paris is eager to marry Juliet, and Old
Capulet invites him to meet her at a family
ball. The Servant who should deliver the
invitations asks Romeo and Benvolio to
read them for him—which gives Benvolio
an idea.

1 *bound*: bound over to keep the peace.
2 *In . . . alike*: or else pay the same
penalty.

4 *honourable reckoning*: (a) good age;
(b) good reputation.
5 *at odds*: as enemies.
6 *suit*: request.

7 *But . . . o'er*: only repeating.
11 *Ere*: before.
*ripe*: ready.
12 *Younger . . . made*: girls younger than
Juliet have become happy mothers.
13 *marr'd*: spoiled; Capulet echoes an old
proverbial saying, 'Soon married, soon
marred'.
14 *Earth . . . she*: all my other children
are dead and buried.
15 *She . . . earth*: Juliet is the only hope
of Capulet's *life*, the only child of his
*body*, and the sole heir of his *estate*;
Capulet plays on different meanings of
'earth'.
17 *My will . . . part*: my wish is in
proportion to her consent.
18 *And she agreed*: once she has agreed.
18–19 *within . . . voice*: my consent and
willing agreement ('fair according
voice') falls within the range of her
choice—i.e. I will accept whoever she
chooses.
20 *old accustom'd*: according to old
custom (see Extracts from *Romeus
and Juliet*, page 122).
22 *store*: number.
25 *Earth-treading stars*: ladies as bright
as stars, yet walking on earth.
26 *lusty*: vigorous.
27 *well-apparell'd*: well-dressed (i.e. in
spring flowers).
28 *limping*: slow-footed.
29 *fennel*: The fragrant yellow flowers of
this plant were believed to awaken
passion.

## SCENE 2

*A street: enter* Capulet, County Paris, *and the*
Clown, Servant *to* Capulet

**Capulet**
But Montague is bound as well as I,
In penalty alike, and 'tis not hard, I think,
For men so old as we to keep the peace.
   **Paris**
Of honourable reckoning are you both,
5 And pity 'tis, you liv'd at odds so long.
But now, my lord, what say you to my suit?
   **Capulet**
But saying o'er what I have said before:
My child is yet a stranger in the world,
She hath not seen the change of fourteen years;
10 Let two more summers wither in their pride,
Ere we may think her ripe to be a bride.
   **Paris**
Younger than she are happy mothers made.
   **Capulet**
And too soon marr'd are those so early made.
Earth hath swallow'd all my hopes but she;
15 She's the hopeful lady of my earth.
But woo her, gentle Paris, get her heart,
My will to her consent is but a part;
And she agreed, within her scope of choice
Lies my consent and fair according voice.
20 This night I hold an old accustom'd feast,
Whereto I have invited many a guest,
Such as I love, and you among the store,
One more, most welcome, makes my number more.
At my poor house look to behold this night
25 Earth-treading stars that make dark heaven light.
Such comfort as do lusty young men feel
When well-apparell'd April on the heel
Of limping winter treads, even such delight
Among fresh fennel buds shall you this night
30 Inherit at my house; hear all, all see;
And like her most whose merit most shall be;

30  *Inherit*: possess.
32–3  *Which . . . number*: and when you have had a look at many girls, mine may prove to be the number one among them.
33  *though . . . none*: although one isn't really a number, mathematically speaking (Capulet makes a little joke).

37  *stay*: wait.

38–41  *It is . . . nets*: Shakespeare parodies the style of a popular prose narrative of the 1580s, John Lyly's *Euphues* ('The shoemaker must not go above his latchet, nor the hedger meddle with anything but his bill . . . ').
39  *yard*: measuring-rod (with a play on 'yard' = penis).
40  *last*: model foot for making or mending shoes.
41  *nets*: i.e. for catching fish.
42  *writ*: written.
44  *learned*: learnèd; i.e. someone who can read.
    *In good time*: just at the right moment.
45–50  *one fire . . . die*: Benvolio offers a selection of proverbial comforts.
47  *holp*: helped.
48  *cures . . . languish*: is cured by suffering from another one.
49  *Take . . . eye*: i.e. look at some other girl.
50  *rank*: foul.
51–2  *Your . . . shin*: Romeo scorns Benvolio's remedies, which treat a broken heart as though it were a scratched leg (which could be given first-aid treatment with the broad leaf of a plantain).

54–6  *bound . . . tormented*: Elizabethan treatments for the insane: Romeo cannot get to see his mistress (his 'food'), and he is the victim of his own thoughts.
56  *God-den*: good evening (a greeting used at any time after twelve noon).
57  *God gi' god-den*: God give you good evening.

Which on more view of many, mine, being one,
May stand in number, though in reck'ning none.
Come go with me. [*To* Servant] Go, sirrah, trudge about
35  Through fair Verona, find those persons out
Whose names are written there [*Gives a paper*], and to them say,
My house and welcome on their pleasure stay.
                                    [*Exit with* Paris

**Servant**
Find them out whose names are written here! It is written that the shoemaker should meddle with his yard
40  and the tailor with his last, the fisher with his pencil and the painter with his nets; but I am sent to find those persons whose names are here writ, and can never find what names the writing person hath here writ. I must to the learned. In good time!

*Enter* Benvolio *and* Romeo

**Benvolio**
45  Tut, man, one fire burns out another's burning,
One pain is lessen'd by another's anguish;
Turn giddy, and be holp by backward turning;
One desperate grief cures with another's languish:
Take thou some new infection to thy eye,
50  And the rank poison of the old will die.
**Romeo**
Your plantain leaf is excellent for that.
**Benvolio**
For what, I pray thee?
**Romeo**
                                    For your broken shin.
**Benvolio**
Why, Romeo, art thou mad?
**Romeo**
Not mad, but bound more than a madman is:
55  Shut up in prison, kept without my food,
Whipt and tormented, and—God-den, good fellow.
**Servant**
God gi' god-den. I pray, sir, can you read?

58 *mine . . . misery*: my own fate in my
   unhappiness; perhaps Romeo means
   that his love will be the cause of his
   death.
59 *without book*: by heart.

62 *Ye say . . . merry*: you're an honest
   man, may God keep you well; the
   servant thinks Romeo is saying that he
   cannot read.

65 *County*: the count.

82 *crush*: drink.

**Romeo**
Ay, mine own fortune in my misery.
   **Servant**
Perhaps you have learned it without book; but I pray,
60 can you read any thing you see?
   **Romeo**
Ay, if I know the letters and the language.
   **Servant**
Ye say honestly, rest you merry.
   **Romeo**
Stay, fellow, I can read.

*He reads the letter*

   'Signior Martino and his wife and daughters,
65   County Anselme and his beauteous sisters,
   The lady widow of Vitruvio,
   Signior Placentio and his lovely nieces,
   Mercutio and his brother Valentine,
   Mine uncle Capulet, his wife and daughters,
70   My fair niece Rosaline, and Livia,
   Signior Valentio and his cousin Tybalt,
   Lucio and the lively Helena.'
A fair assembly: whither should they come?
   **Servant**
Up.
   **Romeo**
75 Whither? to supper?
   **Servant**
To our house.
   **Romeo**
Whose house?
   **Servant**
My master's.
   **Romeo**
Indeed I should have asked thee that before.
   **Servant**
80 Now I'll tell you without asking. My master is the great
rich Capulet, and if you be not of the house of
Montagues, I pray come and crush a cup of wine. Rest
you merry.                                    [*Exit*

84 *ancient*: customary.

86 *admired*: admirèd.

87 *attainted*: not infected (see line 49),
   unprejudiced.

89 *think . . . crow*: Swans are white and
   beautiful; crows are black and ugly.

90–1 *When . . . falsehood*: when my eyes
   switch their religion to believe such
   lies.
92 *these*: i.e. his eyes.
   *drown'd*: drowned in tears.
93 *Transparent*: self-evident; clear.
   *heretics*: people with unorthodox
   religious beliefs (who were often
   burned to death for their beliefs).
95 *match*: equal.

97 *pois'd with*: balanced against.
98 *that crystal scales*: Benvolio compares
   Romeo's clear-seeing eyes to the two
   pans of a set of scales.
99 *lady's love*: the love of your lady (i.e.
   Rosaline).
101 *scant*: hardly.

**Benvolio**
At this same ancient feast of Capulet's
85 Sups the fair Rosaline whom thou so loves,
With all the admired beauties of Verona:
Go thither, and with unattainted eye
Compare her face with some that I shall show,
And I will make thee think thy swan a crow.
   **Romeo**
90 When the devout religion of mine eye
Maintains such falsehood, then turn tears to fires;
And these who, often drown'd, could never die,
Transparent heretics, be burnt for liars.
One fairer than my love! the all-seeing sun
95 Ne'er saw her match since first the world begun.
   **Benvolio**
Tut, you saw her fair, none else being by,
Herself pois'd with herself in either eye;
But in that crystal scales let there be weigh'd
Your lady's love against some other maid
100 That I will show you shining at this feast,
And she shall scant show well that now seems best.
   **Romeo**
I'll go along no such sight to be shown,
But to rejoice in splendour of mine own.        [*Exeunt*

**Act 1 Scene 3**
Lady Capulet tells Juliet and her Nurse
about Paris and his proposal of marriage.

2 *at twelve year old*: The Nurse perhaps
lost her virginity soon after this.
3 *ladybird*: The Nurse's term of
endearment.
4 *God forbid*: i.e. that anything has
happened to Juliet.

7 *what is your will*: what do you want.

8 *give leave awhile*: leave us for a time.

10 *thou s'*: you shall.
*counsel*: conversation.
11 *of a pretty age*: (a) at an attractive
age; (b) old enough.
12 *Faith*: by my faith.

13 *lay*: wager.
14 *teen*: sorrow.
*be it spoken*: it must be said.

16 *Lammas-tide*: 1 August; Lammas
(from an Anglo-Saxon word for 'loaf')
was a harvest festival celebrating the
first ripe corn.
*tide*: time.
*odd*: a few.

18 *Lammas-eve*: 31 July, the day before
Lammas.
19 *Susan*: The Nurse's own daughter.

# SCENE 3

*Sunday afternoon:* Capulet's house. Enter Capulet's
Wife *and* Nurse

**Lady Capulet**
Nurse, where's my daughter? call her forth to me.
**Nurse**
Now by my maidenhead at twelve year old,
I bade her come. What, lamb! What, ladybird!
God forbid, where's this girl? What, Juliet?

*Enter* Juliet

**Juliet**
5 How now, who calls?
**Nurse**
Your mother.
**Juliet**
Madam, I am here, what is your will?
**Lady Capulet**
This is the matter. Nurse, give leave a while,
We must talk in secret. Nurse, come back again,
10 I have remember'd me, thou s' hear our counsel.
Thou knowest my daughter's of a pretty age.
**Nurse**
Faith, I can tell her age unto an hour.
**Lady Capulet**
She's not fourteen.
**Nurse**
              I'll lay fourteen of my teeth—
And yet to my teen be it spoken, I have but four—
15 She's not fourteen. How long is it now
To Lammas-tide?
**Lady Capulet**
             A fortnight and odd days.
**Nurse**
Even or odd, of all days in the year,
Come Lammas-eve at night shall she be fourteen.
Susan and she—God rest all Christian souls!—

20  *of an age*: the same age.
    *with God*: dead.

23  *marry*: by the Virgin Mary.

27  *wormwood*: a bitter herbal preparation
    (used to persuade the infant to stop
    suckling).
    *dug*: breast.
30  *bear a brain*: have a good memory.
31  *it*: the baby, Juliet.

33  *tetchy*: irritable.
34  *'Shake!'*: move, get away.
34–5  *'twas . . . trudge*: there was no need
    to tell me to take myself off.

37  *high-lone*: upright by herself.
    *th'rood*: the cross of Christ.
38  *all about*: everywhere.
39  *broke her brow*: cut her forehead.

41  *'A*: he.
    *took up*: picked up.
42  *quoth*: said.
43  *wit*: sense.
44  *holidam*: holiness.
45  *left*: stopped.
46  *jest*: joke.
    *come about*: come true.
47  *I warrant*: I'm sure.
    *and*: if.
49  *stinted*: stopped (crying).

50  *hold thy peace*: be quiet.

53  *it brow*: its forehead.
54  *stone*: testicle.

57  *comest to age*: are old enough.

20  Were of an age. Well, Susan is with God,
    She was too good for me. But as I said,
    On Lammas-eve at night shall she be fourteen,
    That shall she, marry, I remember it well.
    'Tis since the earthquake now aleven years,
25  And she was wean'd—I never shall forget it—
    Of all the days of the year, upon that day;
    For I had then laid wormwood to my dug,
    Sitting in the sun under the dove-house wall.
    My lord and you were then at Mantua—
30  Nay, I do bear a brain—but as I said,
    When it did taste the wormwood on the nipple
    Of my dug, and felt it bitter, pretty fool,
    To see it tetchy and fall out wi'th'dug!
    'Shake!' quoth the dove-house; 'twas no need, I trow,
35  To bid me trudge.
    And since that time it is aleven years,
    For then she could stand high-lone; nay, by th'rood,
    She could have run and waddled all about;
    For even the day before, she broke her brow,
40  And then my husband—God be with his soul,
    'A was a merry man—took up the child.
    'Yea', quoth he, 'dost thou fall upon thy face?
    Thou wilt fall backward when thou hast more wit,
    Wilt thou not, Jule?' And by my holidam,
45  The pretty wretch left crying, and said 'Ay'.
    To see now how a jest shall come about!
    I warrant, and I should live a thousand years,
    I never should forget it: 'Wilt thou not, Jule?' quoth he,
    And, pretty fool, it stinted, and said 'Ay'.
        **Lady Capulet**
50  Enough of this, I pray thee hold thy peace.
        **Nurse**
    Yes, madam, yet I cannot choose but laugh,
    To think it should leave crying, and say 'Ay':
    And yet I warrant it had upon it brow
    A bump as big as a young cock'rel's stone,
55  A perilous knock, and it cried bitterly.
    'Yea', quoth my husband, 'fall'st upon thy face?
    Thou wilt fall backward when thou comest to age,
    Wilt thou not, Jule?' It stinted, and said 'Ay'.

**Juliet**
And stint thou too, I pray thee, Nurse, say I.
**Nurse**
60  Peace, I have done. God mark thee to his grace,
Thou wast the prettiest babe that e'er I nurs'd.
And I might live to see thee married once,
I have my wish.
**Lady Capulet**
Marry, that 'marry' is the very theme
65  I came to talk of. Tell me, daughter Juliet,
How stands your dispositions to be married?
**Juliet**
It is an honour that I dream not of.
**Nurse**
An honour! were not I thine only nurse,
I would say thou hadst suck'd wisdom from thy teat.
**Lady Capulet**
70  Well, think of marriage now; younger than you,
Here in Verona, ladies of esteem,
Are made already mothers. By my count,
I was your mother much upon these years
That you are now a maid. Thus then in brief:
75  The valiant Paris seeks you for his love.
**Nurse**
A man, young lady! lady, such a man
As all the world—Why, he's a man of wax.
**Lady Capulet**
Verona's summer hath not such a flower.
**Nurse**
Nay, he's a flower, in faith, a very flower.
**Lady Capulet**
80  What say you, can you love the gentleman?
This night you shall behold him at our feast;
Read o'er the volume of young Paris' face,
And find delight writ there with beauty's pen;
Examine every married lineament,
85  And see how one another lends content;
And what obscur'd in this fair volume lies
Find written in the margent of his eyes.
This precious book of love, this unbound lover,
To beautify him, only lacks a cover.

---

**Notes (left column):**

60 *God . . . grace*: may God choose you for His special grace.

62–3 *And . . . wish*: if I could live to see you married, I should have all I could wish for.

66 *How . . . married*: how do you feel about being married.

68 *were . . . nurse*: if I were not the only nurse who has fed you.

71 *ladies of esteem*: noble ladies.

72 *count*: reckoning.

73 *much upon these years*: at about the same age.

77 *a man of wax*: a perfect model of a man.

79 *in faith*: indeed.

82–93 *Read . . . story*: Lady Capulet's extended simile describes Paris in terms of an expensive book.

82 *volume*: part of a book (as the face is part of the whole man).

83 *writ*: written.

84 *married*: harmoniously united. *lineament*: line (in a book); feature (in the face).

85 *one . . . content*: each feature fits in with the others.

86–7 *what . . . eyes*: what you cannot read in his face will be written, like marginal notes, in his eyes.

88 *unbound*: without a cover (the book); unmarried (the man).

90 *The fish . . . sea*: a fish is in its own element in the sea; Lady Capulet perhaps suggests that marriage is the proper element for a man.

90–1 *'tis . . . hide*: it's very fitting that a handsome man ('the fair within') should have a beautiful wife.

92 *in many's eyes*: in the opinion of many people.

93 *clasps*: fasteners; embraces.

95 *no less*: no lower (in social esteem).

96 *grow*: i.e. become pregnant.

97 *like of*: be pleased with.

98 *I'll . . . like*: I'll expect to like him. *if looking . . . move*: if seeing him is enough to make me like him.

99–100 *no more . . . fly*: I won't give him any more encouragement than you will allow.

99 *endart*: shoot as a dart.

103 *in extremity*: in a terrible mess.

104 *to wait*: to serve food and drink. *straight*: immediately.

105 *the County stays*: Count Paris is waiting for you.

90 The fish lives in the sea, and 'tis much pride
For fair without the fair within to hide;
That book in many's eyes doth share the glory
That in gold clasps locks in the golden story:
So shall you share all that he doth possess,
95 By having him, making yourself no less.
    **Nurse**
No less! nay, bigger women grow by men.
    **Lady Capulet**
Speak briefly, can you like of Paris' love?
    **Juliet**
I'll look to like, if looking liking move;
But no more deep will I endart mine eye
100 Than your consent gives strength to make it fly.

*Enter* Servingman

    **Servingman**
Madam, the guests are come, supper served up, you called, my young lady asked for, the Nurse cursed in the pantry, and every thing in extremity. I must hence to wait, I beseech you follow straight.     [*Exit*
    **Lady Capulet**
105 We follow thee. Juliet, the County stays.
    **Nurse**
Go, girl, seek happy nights to happy days.     [*Exeunt*

**Act 1 Scene 4**
Benvolio and Mercutio persuade Romeo to
join them in a masquerade.

1  *shall . . . excuse*: shall we make a
   speech to explain ourselves; such
   masked intruders usually offered a
   prepared speech, complimenting the
   host and flattering his guests.
   *spoke*: spoken.
2  *shall we on*: shall we go on.
3  *The date . . . prolixity*: such
   longwindedness is out of date.
4–8  *We'll . . . entrance*: Benvolio rejects
   the old-fashioned style of presenting a
   masquerade.
4–5  *no Cupid . . . lath*: no blindfolded
   Cupid carrying a Tartar's bow made of
   painted wood—see *1, 1, 165* and
   illustration.
6  *crow-keeper*: scarecrow.
7  *without-book prologue*: prologue
   spoken from memory.
   *faintly*: hesitantly, in a low voice.
8  *After the prompter*: following the
   prompter (because the speaker has
   forgotten his lines).
9  *measure*: judge.
10  *measure . . . measure*: tread out some
   stately dance for them.
11  *for this ambling*: in favour of this
   prancing about.
12  *heavy*: gloomy, melancholy.
16  *stakes*: fixes.
18  *above a common bound*: out of the
   ordinary way.

19  *sore*: painfully.
   *enpierced*: enpiercèd; pierced
   through.
   *shaft*: arrow.
21  *bound a pitch*: soar to a height from
   which a hawk stoops to kill.

23  *to sink . . . love*: if you cannot rise to
   the occasion, you will be a burden on
   the one you love.

# SCENE 4

*Sunday evening: outside* Capulet's *house. Enter*
Romeo, Mercutio, Benvolio, *with five or six other*
Maskers, Torch-bearers

**Romeo**
What, shall this speech be spoke for our excuse?
Or shall we on without apology?
    **Benvolio**
The date is out of such prolixity:
We'll have no Cupid hoodwink'd with a scarf,
5  Bearing a Tartar's painted bow of lath,
Scaring the ladies like a crow-keeper,
Nor no without-book prologue, faintly spoke
After the prompter, for our entrance;
But let them measure us by what they will,
10  We'll measure them a measure and be gone.
    **Romeo**
Give me a torch, I am not for this ambling;
Being but heavy, I will bear the light.
    **Mercutio**
Nay, gentle Romeo, we must have you dance.
    **Romeo**
Not I, believe me. You have dancing shoes
15  With nimble soles, I have a soul of lead
So stakes me to the ground I cannot move.
    **Mercutio**
You are a lover, borrow Cupid's wings,
And soar with them above a common bound.
    **Romeo**
I am too sore enpierced with his shaft
20  To soar with his light feathers, and so bound
I cannot bound a pitch above dull woe:
Under love's heavy burden do I sink.
    **Mercutio**
And to sink in it should you burden love,
Too great oppression for a tender thing.
    **Romeo**
25  Is love a tender thing? it is too rough,
Too rude, too boist'rous, and it pricks like thorn.

28 *Prick . . . down*: get your own back on
   love, and you will defeat it; stimulate
   love into action, and you will deflate
   desire.

29 *case*: cover, mask.
   *visage*: face.

30 *A visor . . . visor*: an ugly mask for an
   ugly face.

31 *curious*: inquisitive.
   *cote*: observe.

32 *the . . . for me*: Benvolio's mask
   probably has heavy, over-hanging
   eyebrows, and red cheeks.

34 *betake . . . legs*: begin dancing.

36 *senseless rushes*: unfeeling rushes
   (strewn over floors and stages).

37 *I am . . . phrase*: I can quote
   grandfather's old proverb ('A good
   candle-holder proves a good
   gamester'—i.e. the spectator sees the
   best of the game).

39 *The game . . . fair*: the game is at its
   best (and a wise gambler stops
   playing at this point).
   *done*: finished.

40 *dun's the mouse*: the mouse is brown
   ('dun'); Mercutio quibbles on Romeo's
   'done' with the watchword (meaning
   'be quiet and secret') suitable for a
   constable on night patrol.

41 *If . . . mire*: 'Dun-in-the-mire' (stick-
   in-the-mud) was a winter game where
   players tried to pull a log representing
   the carthorse 'Dun' out of imaginary
   mud.

42 *save your reverence*: excuse me;
   Mercutio makes a mock-apology for
   indecency.

43 *burn daylight*: waste time.

44 *that's not so*: Romeo pretends to
   misunderstand Mercutio's meaning.

**Mercutio**
If love be rough with you, be rough with love:
Prick love for pricking, and you beat love down.
Give me a case to put my visage in, [*Puts on a mask*]
30  A visor for a visor! what care I
What curious eye doth cote deformities?
Here are the beetle brows shall blush for me.
   **Benvolio**
Come knock and enter, and no sooner in,
But every man betake him to his legs.
   **Romeo**
35  A torch for me: let wantons light of heart
Tickle the senseless rushes with their heels;
For I am proverb'd with a grandsire phrase,
I'll be a candle-holder and look on:
The game was ne'er so fair, and I am done.
   **Mercutio**
40  Tut, dun's the mouse, the constable's own word.
If thou art Dun, we'll draw thee from the mire,
Or (save your reverence) love, wherein thou stickest
Up to the ears. Come, we burn daylight, ho!
   **Romeo**
Nay, that's not so.
   **Mercutio**
               I mean, sir, in delay
45  We waste our lights in vain, like lights by day.

46–7 *Take . . . wits*: accept our true meaning, which is five times more trustworthy than impressions received through the five senses ('wits').

48 *mean well*: have good intentions. *mask*: masquerade, disguising.

49 *wit*: sense.

52 *while*: somewhile, sometimes.

53 *Queen Mab*: A fantastic creation of Shakespeare's own imagination, with no known counterpart in other fairy literature.

54 *fairies' midwife*: the fairy responsible for delivering the creations of the sleeping imagination ('the children of an idle brain'—line 97).

55 *agate-stone*: i.e. a figure carved in agate, set in a seal-ring.

57 *atomi*: tiny creatures, small as atoms.

60 *joiner*: carpenter; squirrels have sharp teeth, and gnaw through wood. *old grub*: mature larva (especially of a beetle), which bore holes inside nuts.

61 *Time out a'mind*: from time immemorial.

62 *waggon-spokes*: the spokes of the wheels. *spinners*: spiders.

63 *cover*: canopy, hood.

64 *traces*: harness.

65 *Her . . . beams*: The 'team of little atomi' must somehow be harnessed to the chariot—but Mercutio seems to be describing the *shafts* rather than 'collars'.

66 *film*: gossamer (the thread of spiders' webs).

68–9 *worm . . . maid*: Little worms were said to breed in the fingers of lazy maid-servants.

70 *state*: splendour.

72 *cur'sies*: bending the knee as a sign of respect; courtesy.

73 *straight*: immediately.

Take our good meaning, for our judgement sits
Five times in that ere once in our five wits.
   **Romeo**
And we mean well in going to this mask,
But 'tis no wit to go.
   **Mercutio**
                  Why, may one ask?
   **Romeo**
50 I dreamt a dream tonight.
   **Mercutio**
                    And so did I.
   **Romeo**
Well, what was yours?
   **Mercutio**
                     That dreamers often lie.
   **Romeo**
In bed asleep, while they do dream things true.
   **Mercutio**
O then I see Queen Mab hath been with you:
She is the fairies' midwife, and she comes
55 In shape no bigger than an agate-stone
On the forefinger of an alderman,
Drawn with a team of little atomi
Over men's noses as they lie asleep.
Her chariot is an empty hazel-nut,
60 Made by the joiner squirrel or old grub,
Time out a'mind the fairies' coachmakers:
Her waggon-spokes made of long spinners' legs,
The cover of the wings of grasshoppers,
Her traces of the smallest spider web,
65 Her collars of the moonshine's wat'ry beams,
Her whip of cricket's bone, the lash of film,
Her waggoner a small grey-coated gnat,
Not half so big as a round little worm
Prick'd from the lazy finger of a maid.
70 And in this state she gallops night by night
Through lovers' brains, and then they dream of love,
O'er courtiers' knees, that dream on cur'sies straight,
O'er lawyers' fingers, who straight dream on fees,
O'er ladies' lips, who straight on kisses dream,
75 Which oft the angry Mab with blisters plagues,

78 *smelling out a suit*: finding a case to
present in a court of law.
79 *a tithe-pig*: a pig due as 'tithe' (= a
tenth part of someone's income) to
the church, paying part of the parson's
salary.
80 *'a*: he.
81 *another benefice*: a second church
appointment (in addition to the one
he has already).
84 *breaches*: breaking down defences.
*ambuscadoes*: ambushes.
*Spanish blades*: the best swords,
made in Spain from Toledo steel.
85 *healths . . . deep*: very heavy drinking.
*anon*: at once.
86 *starts*: is startled.
88 *very*: same.
89 *plats the manes*: makes the manes
knotted and untidy.
90 *bakes . . . hairs*: cakes the dirty hair of
slovenly wenches; such tangles were
thought to be the work of elves.
91 *once . . . bodes*: will bring even
more misfortune until they are
untangled once and for all.
92 *hag*: witch.
93 *learns*: teaches.
*bear*: (a) bear weight on their bodies;
(b) bear children.
94 *carriage*: posture.

98 *vain*: empty.

101 *Even now*: at one moment.
*bosom*: heart.
102 *anger'd*: i.e. because the frozen north
remains cold.
103 *Turning his side*: changing direction.
104 *from ourselves*: from our real purpose.

106 *misgives*: warns.
107 *yet . . . stars*: ordained by the stars,
but not yet revealed.
109 *expire*: put an end to.
*term*: period.

Because their breaths with sweetmeats tainted are.
Sometime she gallops o'er a courtier's nose,
And then dreams he of smelling out a suit;
And sometime comes she with a tithe-pig's tail
80 Tickling a parson's nose as 'a lies asleep,
Then he dreams of another benefice.
Sometime she driveth o'er a soldier's neck,
And then dreams he of cutting foreign throats,
Of breaches, ambuscadoes, Spanish blades,
85 Of healths five fathom deep; and then anon
Drums in his ear, at which he starts and wakes,
And being thus frighted, swears a prayer or two,
And sleeps again. This is that very Mab
That plats the manes of horses in the night,
90 And bakes the elf-locks in foul sluttish hairs,
Which, once untangl'd, much misfortune bodes.
This is the hag, when maids lie on their backs,
That presses them and learns them first to bear,
Making them women of good carriage.
95 This is she—
    **Romeo**
            Peace, peace, Mercutio, peace!
Thou talk'st of nothing.
    **Mercutio**
                True, I talk of dreams,
Which are the children of an idle brain,
Begot of nothing but vain fantasy,
Which is as thin of substance as the air,
100 And more inconstant than the wind, who woos
Even now the frozen bosom of the north,
And being anger'd puffs away from thence,
Turning his side to the dew-dropping south.
    **Benvolio**
This wind you talk of blows us from ourselves:
105 Supper is done, and we shall come too late.
    **Romeo**
I fear too early, for my mind misgives
Some consequence yet hanging in the stars
Shall bitterly begin his fearful date
With this night's revels, and expire the term

110 *despised*: despisèd.
  *clos'd*: enclosed.
111 *forfeit*: payment.
  *untimely*: early.
112 *steerage*: directing, responsibility for steering.
113 *sail*: which way I sail.
114 *Strike, drum*: Benvolio speaks to the drummer who is leading the group of revellers.

**Act 1 Scene 5**
Love at first sight: Romeo meets Juliet. Tybalt wants to start a fight, but Capulet restrains him. Juliet questions her Nurse about the unknown young man.

1 *take away*: remove the dishes.
2 *trencher*: plate.

5 *join-stools*: stools made by a carpenter.
  *court-cupboard*: sideboard.
6 *look to the plate*: keep an eye on the silver.
  *Good thou*: be a good chap.
7 *marchpane*: marzipan.
  *as*: if.
  *let the porter*: tell the porter.

12 *great chamber*: main hall.

14 *the longer liver*: the one who lives longest.

---

110 Of a despised life clos'd in my breast,
By some vile forfeit of untimely death.
But He that hath the steerage of my course
Direct my sail! On, lusty gentlemen.
**Benvolio**
Strike, drum.

*They march about the stage and stand to one side*

## SCENE 5

*Sunday night: Capulet's house. And* Servingmen *come forth with napkins*

**First Servingman**
Where's Potpan, that he helps not to take away? He shift a trencher? he scrape a trencher?
**Second Servingman**
When good manners shall lie all in one or two men's hands, and they unwashed too, 'tis a foul thing.
**First Servingman**
5 Away with the join-stools, remove the court-cupboard, look to the plate. Good thou, save me a piece of marchpane, and as thou loves me, let the porter let in Susan Grindstone and Nell.
[*Exit* Second Servingman
Anthony and Potpan!

*Enter two more* Servingmen

**Third Servingman**
10 Ay, boy, ready.
**First Servingman**
You are looked for and called for, asked for and sought for, in the great chamber.
**Fourth Servingman**
We cannot be here and there too. Cheerly, boys, be brisk a while, and the longer liver take all.

*They retire behind*

*Enter* Capulet, Lady Capulet, Juliet, Tybalt *and his*
Page, Nurse, *and all the* Guests *and* Gentlewomen *to*
*the Maskers*

**Capulet**

15 Welcome, gentlemen! Ladies that have toes
Unplagu'd with corns will walk a bout with you.
Ah, my mistresses, which of you all
Will now deny to dance? She that makes dainty,
She I'll swear hath corns. Am I come near ye now?
20 Welcome, gentlemen! I have seen the day
That I have worn a visor and could tell
A whispering tale in a fair lady's ear,
Such as would please; 'tis gone, 'tis gone, 'tis gone.
You are welcome, gentlemen. Come, musicians, play.

*Music plays*

25 A hall, a hall, give room! and foot it, girls.

*And they dance*

More light, you knaves, and turn the tables up;
And quench the fire, the room is grown too hot.
Ah, sirrah, this unlook'd-for sport comes well.
Nay, sit, nay, sit, good Cousin Capulet,
30 For you and I are past our dancing days.
How long is't now since last yourself and I
Were in a mask?
**Cousin Capulet**
                        Berlady, thirty years.
**Capulet**
What, man, 'tis not so much, 'tis not so much:
'Tis since the nuptial of Lucentio,
35 Come Pentecost as quickly as it will,
Some five and twenty years, and then we mask'd.
**Cousin Capulet**
'Tis more, 'tis more, his son is elder, sir;
His son is thirty.

16 *walk a bout*: have a dance.

18 *deny*: refuse.
*makes dainty*: makes a fuss.
19 *Am . . . ye*: have I guessed the truth
about you.
21 *visor*: mask.

25 *A hall*: make room.
*foot it*: get on with the dancing.

26 *knaves*: fellows.
*turn . . . up*: i.e. remove the boards
and tidy away the trestles.
28 *Ah, sirrah*: Capulet congratulates
himself.
*unlook'd-for*: unexpected;
Shakespeare has forgotten that this is
an 'old accustom'd feast' (*1*, 2, 20).
29 *Cousin Capulet*: i.e. the 'uncle
Capulet' of the invitation (*1*, 2, 69).
32 *in a mask*: in a masquerade; wearing a
mask.
33 *Berlady*: by Our Lady (the Virgin
Mary).

34 *nuptial*: wedding.
35 *Pentecost*: Whitsuntide.

37 *elder*: older.

38 *Will . . . that*: you don't say so!
39 *but*: only.
  *a ward*: under the control of a guardian, a minor.
40 *enrich the hand*: make the hand richer (i.e. by holding it).

42 *I . . . not*: Perhaps the Servingman is not one of Capulet's regular servants.

45 *Ethiop*: African.
46 *Beauty . . . dear*: beauty that is too precious for everyday use, and too valuable for this world.
47 *shows*: appears.
49 *The measure done*: when this dance is ended.
  *place of stand*: where she stands.
50 *blessed*: blessèd.
  *rude*: rough.
51 *forswear*: deny.

55 *antic face*: comic mask.
56 *fleer*: sneer.
  *solemnity*: ceremony.
57 *stock and honour*: honourable breeding.
  *kin*: family.
58 *hold*: consider.

61 *spite*: contempt.

64 *Content thee*: calm yourself.
  *coz*: cousin; the term was used affectionately to refer to *any* relative.
65 *portly*: dignified.

**Capulet**
　　　　　Will you tell me that?
His son was but a ward two years ago.
　**Romeo**
40 [*To a* Servingman] What lady's that which doth enrich the hand
Of yonder knight?
　**Servingman**
I know not, sir.
　**Romeo**
O she doth teach the torches to burn bright!
It seems she hangs upon the cheek of night
45 As a rich jewel in an Ethiop's ear—
Beauty too rich for use, for earth too dear:
So shows a snowy dove trooping with crows,
As yonder lady o'er her fellows shows.
The measure done, I'll watch her place of stand,
50 And touching hers, make blessed my rude hand.
Did my heart love till now? forswear it, sight!
For I ne'er saw true beauty till this night.
　**Tybalt**
This, by his voice, should be a Montague.
Fetch me my rapier, boy.　　　　　[*Exit* Page
　　　　　　　　　What dares the slave
55 Come hither, cover'd with an antic face,
To fleer and scorn at our solemnity?
Now by the stock and honour of my kin,
To strike him dead I hold it not a sin.
　**Capulet**
Why, how now, kinsman, wherefore storm you so?
　**Tybalt**
60 Uncle, this is a Montague, our foe:
A villain that is hither come in spite,
To scorn at our solemnity this night.
　**Capulet**
Young Romeo is it?
　**Tybalt**
　　　　　'Tis he, that villain Romeo.
　**Capulet**
Content thee, gentle coz, let him alone,
65 'A bears him like a portly gentleman;

66  *to say truth*: indeed.
    *brags of*: boasts about.
67  *well-govern'd*: good mannered.

69  *do him disparagement*: dishonour
    him.

72  *Show a fair presence*: behave in a
    friendly manner.
73  *ill-beseeming semblance*: unsuitable
    appearance.

76  *goodman boy*: unmannerly child.
    *go to*: shame on you (an expression of
    impatience).
79  *make a mutiny*: start a fight.
80  *set cock-a-hoop*: cause disorder.
    *be the man*: give the orders.
81  *shame*: dishonour.
83  *This . . . you*: this behaviour may
    perhaps damage your [financial]
    expectations.
    *I know what*: i.e. I can see that it
    does.
84  *contrary me*: oppose my will.
84–7  *Marry . . . hearts*: Capulet speaks to
    his guests, and then (privately) to
    Tybalt.
85  *princox*: insolent young man.
87  *Cheerly*: heartily.
88–9  *Patience . . . greeting*: enforced
    patience meeting with obstinate anger
    in a clash of opposites ('different
    greeting') sets my whole body
    trembling.
90  *withdraw*: leave the room.
91  *gall*: bitterness.
92–105  *If I . . . I take*: The formal
    patterning of these fourteen lines (a
    sonnet) isolates the lovers from
    Capulet's other guests, and
    emphasizes the special moment of
    their first meeting.
93  *This holy shrine*: i.e. Juliet's hand.
96–9  *Good pilgrim . . . kiss*: Juliet
    immediately responds to Romeo's
    approach, sharing his image and
    matching the four rhyming lines of his
    quatrain.
97  *Which . . . this*: which shows proper
    respect in what it is doing (i.e.
    touching my hand).

And to say truth, Verona brags of him
To be a virtuous and well-govern'd youth.
I would not for the wealth of all this town
Here in my house do him disparagement;
70  Therefore be patient, take no note of him;
It is my will, the which if thou respect,
Show a fair presence, and put off these frowns,
An ill-beseeming semblance for a feast.
   **Tybalt**
It fits when such a villain is a guest:
75  I'll not endure him.
   **Capulet**
                          He shall be endur'd.
What, goodman boy, I say he shall, go to!
Am I the master here, or you? go to!
You'll not endure him? God shall mend my soul,
You'll make a mutiny among my guests!
80  You will set cock-a-hoop! you'll be the man!
   **Tybalt**
Why, uncle, 'tis a shame.
   **Capulet**
                          Go to, go to,
You are a saucy boy. Is't so indeed?
This trick may chance to scathe you, I know what.
You must contrary me! Marry, 'tis time.—
85  Well said, my hearts!—You are a princox, go,
Be quiet, or—More light, more light!—For shame,
I'll make you quiet, what!—Cheerly, my hearts!
   **Tybalt**
Patience perforce with wilful choler meeting
Makes my flesh tremble in their different greeting:
90  I will withdraw, but this intrusion shall,
Now seeming sweet, convert to bitt'rest gall.        [*Exit*
   **Romeo**
[*To* Juliet] If I profane with my unworthiest hand
This holy shrine, the gentle sin is this,
My lips, two blushing pilgrims, ready stand
95  To smooth that rough touch with a tender kiss.
   **Juliet**
Good pilgrim, you do wrong your hand too much,
Which mannerly devotion shows in this,

98 *saints*: i.e. the images of saints in shrines.
99 *palmers*: pilgrims to Jerusalem (who brought palm leaves back with them).

For saints have hands that pilgrims' hands do touch,
And palm to palm is holy palmers' kiss.
   **Romeo**
100 Have not saints lips, and holy palmers too?
   **Juliet**
Ay, pilgrim, lips that they must use in prayer.
   **Romeo**

102 *let . . . do*: allow lips the same privilege (i.e. in kissing) as hands.
103 *grant thou*: grant their prayers.

O then, dear saint, let lips do what hands do:
They pray, grant thou, lest faith turn to despair.
   **Juliet**

104 *move*: take the initiative (i.e. Romeo must take the first step himself and kiss Juliet).
105 *move not*: stand still.
   *effect*: result (i.e. a kiss).

Saints do not move, though grant for prayers' sake.
   **Romeo**
105 Then move not while my prayer's effect I take.
Thus from my lips, by thine, my sin is purg'd.

*Kissing her*

   **Juliet**
Then have my lips the sin that they have took.
   **Romeo**

108 *urg'd*: argued.

Sin from my lips? O trespass sweetly urg'd!
Give me my sin again.

*Kissing her again*

   **Juliet**
                    You kiss by th' book.

109 *by the book*: expertly (as though he had studied the subject in a book).

   **Nurse**
110 Madam, your mother craves a word with you.
   **Romeo**
What is her mother?
   **Nurse**

111 *Marry*: by the Virgin Mary.
   *bachelor*: young gentleman.

                    Marry, bachelor,
Her mother is the lady of the house,
And a good lady, and a wise and virtuous.
I nurs'd her daughter that you talk'd withal;

114 *withal*: with.

115 I tell you, he that can lay hold of her
Shall have the chinks.

116 *the chinks*: plenty of money.

   **Romeo**
                    Is she a Capulet?

117 *dear account*: costly reckoning.
   *my . . . debt*: I owe my life to my enemy.

O dear account! my life is my foe's debt.

118 *sport . . . best*: i.e. the proper time to leave it—see *1, 4*, 39note.

**Benvolio**
Away, be gone, the sport is at the best.
**Romeo**
Ay, so I fear, the more is my unrest.
**Capulet**
120 Nay, gentlemen, prepare not to be gone,
We have a trifling foolish banquet towards.

121 *foolish banquet*: simple dessert (fruits, sweets, and wine).
*towards*: about to be served.

*They whisper in his ear*

122 *Is . . . so*: is that what it is (the maskers have made a whispered excuse).
124 *More torches*: i.e. to light the way for the gentlemen.
125 *fay*: faith.
*waxes*: grows.

Is it e'en so? Why then I thank you all.
I thank you, honest gentlemen, good night.
More torches here, come on! then let's to bed.
125 Ah, sirrah, by my fay, it waxes late,
I'll to my rest.      [*Exeunt all but* Juliet *and* Nurse
**Juliet**
Come hither, Nurse. What is yond gentleman?
**Nurse**

127 *yond gentleman*: that gentleman over there; Juliet tries to conceal her special interest in Romeo by asking the Nurse about other young men (see Extracts, page 122).

The son and heir of old Tiberio.
**Juliet**
What's he that now is going out of door?
**Nurse**
130 Marry, that I think be young Petruchio.
**Juliet**
What's he that follows here, that would not dance?
**Nurse**
I know not.
**Juliet**

133 *married*: marrièd.
134 *My grave . . . bed*: I will die if I can't marry him (an ironic anticipation of events to come).
*like*: likely.

Go ask his name.—If he be married,
My grave is like to be my wedding bed.
**Nurse**
135 His name is Romeo, and a Montague,
The only son of your great enemy.
**Juliet**
My only love sprung from my only hate!
Too early seen unknown, and known too late!

139 *Prodigious*: ominous, foretelling evil.
140 *loathed*: loathèd.

Prodigious birth of love it is to me,
140 That I must love a loathed enemy.
**Nurse**
What's tis? what's tis?

**Juliet**
A rhyme I learnt even now
Of one I danc'd withal.

141 *even*: just.

*One calls within, 'Juliet!'*

142s.d. *within*: from offstage.

**Nurse**
Anon, anon!
Come let's away, the strangers all are gone.    [*Exeunt*

142 *Anon*: I'm coming.

*Enter* Chorus

**Chorus**
Now old desire doth in his death-bed lie,
145 And young affection gapes to be his heir;
That fair for which love groan'd for and would die,
With tender Juliet match'd is now not fair.
Now Romeo is belov'd, and loves again,
Alike bewitched by the charm of looks;
150 But to his foe suppos'd he must complain,
And she steal love's sweet bait from fearful hooks.
Being held a foe, he may not have access
To breathe such vows as lovers use to swear,
And she as much in love, her means much less
155 To meet her new-beloved any where:
But passion lends them power, time means, to meet,
Temp'ring extremities with extreme sweet.    [*Exit*

144–57 *Now . . . sweet*: The second
sonnet spoken by the Chorus—now
openly disapproving—is sometimes
taken as a prologue to *Act 2*.
145 *gapes . . . heir*: waits with open mouth
to swallow his inheritance.
146 *That fair*: that fair lady (i.e. Rosaline).
148 *again*: in return.
149 *Alike*: both of them.
*bewitched*: bewitchèd.
150 *foe suppos'd*: the one who was
supposed to be his enemy.
*complain*: lament as a lover.
151 *fearful*: dangerous.
152 *held*: considered to be.
153 *use*: are accustomed.
155 *beloved*: belovèd.
157 *Temp'ring extremities*: softening
extreme hardships.

# ACT 2

**Act 2 Scene 1**
Romeo hides from his friends, who joke
about his love for Rosaline.

## SCENE 1

*Late Sunday night: outside* Capulet's orchard. *Enter*
Romeo *alone*

**Romeo**
Can I go forward when my heart is here?
Turn back, dull earth, and find thy centre out.

Romeo *withdraws*

*Enter* Benvolio *with* Mercutio

**Benvolio**
Romeo! my cousin Romeo! Romeo!
**Mercutio**
                         He is wise,
And on my life hath stol'n him home to bed.
**Benvolio**
5 He ran this way and leapt this orchard wall.
Call, good Mercutio.
**Mercutio**
                Nay, I'll conjure too.
Romeo! humours! madman! passion! lover!
Appear thou in the likeness of a sigh,
Speak but one rhyme, and I am satisfied;
10 Cry but 'Ay me!', pronounce but 'love' and 'dove',
Speak to my gossip Venus one fair word,
One nickname for her purblind son and heir,
Young Abraham Cupid, he that shot so trim
When King Cophetua lov'd the beggar-maid.
15 He heareth not, he stirreth not, he moveth not,
The ape is dead, and I must conjure him.
I conjure thee by Rosaline's bright eyes,
By her high forehead and her scarlet lip,
By her fine foot, straight leg, and quivering thigh,

1 *Can . . . here*: can my body go away
when my heart is here.
2 *earth*: The human body was
traditionally said to be made from 'the
dust of the ground' (Genesis 2:7).
*centre*: heart.

4 *stol'n him*: secretly taken himself.
6 *conjure*: raise him up by magic.
7 *humours*: fantasies.
8 *likeness*: shape; a magician should
always specify the exact form that an
apparition should take.
9 *satisfied*: convinced of the spirit's
identity.
10 *but*: only.
'love' and 'dove': i.e. some of the
typical rhymes of love poetry.
11 *my gossip Venus*: my old friend
Venus—the goddess of love.
12 *purblind*: completely blind.
13 *Young . . . Cupid*: that little beggar
Cupid; Mercutio identifies Cupid with
the 'Abraham men'—half-naked
beggars who cheated the public by
pretending madness.
*trim*: neatly, accurately.
14 *King Cophetua . . . maid*: A popular
Elizabethan ballad tells the story of a
legendary king in Africa who fell in
love with a beggar-maid.
16 *The . . . dead*: Romeo is like a
performing monkey pretending to be
dead.

20 *demesnes*: parklands.
21 *thy likeness*: your own person.

22 *And if*: if.

24 *raise a spirit*: call up a ghost; have an erection.
   *circle*: magic area (in conjuring).
26 *laid it*: satisfied it.
   *conjur'd it down*: dismissed it.
27 *spite*: injury.

31 *consorted*: associated.
   *humorous*: damp; causing melancholy.
32 *befits*: suits.

33 *hit the mark*: achieve its aim.

34 *medlar tree*: tree bearing small, brown-skinned apples which were not ripe for eating until they were ready to burst open with juice.

38 *an open-arse*: a medlar.
   *a pop'rin pear*: a pear named after the Flemish town Poperinghe; a slang term for 'penis'.
39 *truckle-bed*: little bed on castors.
40 *field-bed*: bed in the open air.

**Act 2 Scene 2**
Romeo has lost his heart, and Juliet sighs out her new love, unaware that Romeo is listening. When he reveals himself, they arrange for Juliet's Nurse to act as their go-between.

1 *He . . . wound*: he can laugh at scars because he has never been wounded; the rhyme with Benvolio's 'found' (scene 1, line 42) indicates that no scene break is intended—although Romeo is now *inside* the orchard.

20 And the demesnes that there adjacent lie,
   That in thy likeness thou appear to us.
      **Benvolio**
   And if he hear thee, thou wilt anger him.
      **Mercutio**
   This cannot anger him; 'twould anger him
   To raise a spirit in his mistress' circle,
25 Of some strange nature, letting it there stand
   Till she had laid it and conjur'd it down:
   That were some spite. My invocation
   Is fair and honest: in his mistress' name
   I conjure only but to raise up him.
      **Benvolio**
30 Come, he hath hid himself among these trees
   To be consorted with the humorous night:
   Blind is his love, and best befits the dark.
      **Mercutio**
   If love be blind, love cannot hit the mark.
   Now will he sit under a medlar tree,
35 And wish his mistress were that kind of fruit
   As maids call medlars, when they laugh alone.
   O Romeo, that she were, O that she were
   An open-arse, thou a pop'rin pear!
   Romeo, good night, I'll to my truckle-bed,
40 This field-bed is too cold for me to sleep.
   Come, shall we go?
      **Benvolio**
                    Go then, for 'tis in vain
   To seek him here that means not to be found.
                           [*Exit with* Mercutio

## Scene 2

*Very late Sunday night/early Monday morning:*
*Capulet's orchard.* Romeo *advances*

**Romeo**
He jests at scars that never felt a wound.
But soft, what light through yonder window breaks?
It is the east, and Juliet is the sun.
Arise, fair sun, and kill the envious moon,

6 *her maid*: her votary, dedicated to
Diana (goddess of the moon and
patroness of virgins).

8–9 *Her . . . wear it*: Romeo compares
the habitual 'greensickness'
(= anaemia) of young girls ('vestals'),
to the green and yellow coat worn by
professional jesters.

9s.d. *aloft*: i.e. upon the balcony at the
back of the stage.

11 *O that . . . were*: I wish she knew that
she is the lady I love.

13 *discourses*: speaks eloquently.

17 *spheres*: orbits.

21 *airy region*: sky.
*stream*: shine beams of light.

28 *winged*: wingèd.

29 *white . . . eyes*: eyes showing their
whites as they look in wonder.
*upturned*: upturnèd.

30 *fall back*: throw their heads back.

31 *lazy puffing clouds*: slow-moving puffs
of cloud.

33 *wherefore . . . Romeo*: why is your
name 'Romeo'.

34 *Deny your father*: refuse to
acknowledge your parentage.

5 Who is already sick and pale with grief
That thou, her maid, art far more fair than she.
Be not her maid, since she is envious;
Her vestal livery is but sick and green,
And none but fools do wear it; cast it off.

Juliet *appears aloft as at a window*

10 It is my lady, O it is my love:
O that she knew she were!
She speaks, yet she says nothing; what of that?
Her eye discourses, I will answer it.
I am too bold, 'tis not to me she speaks:
15 Two of the fairest stars in all the heaven,
Having some business, do entreat her eyes,
To twinkle in their spheres till they return.
What if her eyes were there, they in her head?
The brightness of her cheek would shame those stars,
20 As daylight doth a lamp; her eyes in heaven
Would through the airy region stream so bright
That birds would sing and think it were not night.
See how she leans her cheek upon her hand!
O that I were a glove upon that hand,
25 That I might touch that cheek!
    **Juliet**
                                        Ay me!
    **Romeo**
[*Aside*]                               She speaks.
O speak again, bright angel, for thou art
As glorious to this night, being o'er my head,
As is a winged messenger of heaven
Unto the white-upturned wond'ring eyes
30 Of mortals that fall back to gaze on him,
When he bestrides the lazy puffing clouds,
And sails upon the bosom of the air.
    **Juliet**
O Romeo, Romeo, wherefore art thou Romeo?
Deny thy father and refuse thy name;
35 Or if thou wilt not, be but sworn my love,
And I'll no longer be a Capulet.

'Lady, by yonder blessed moon I vow,' (*2*, 2, 107). Michael Thomas as Romeo and Janet Maw as Juliet, Prospect Theatre Company, 1979. Photograph by Zoe Dominic.

**Romeo**
[*Aside*] Shall I hear more, or shall I speak at this?
   **Juliet**
'Tis but thy name that is my enemy;
Thou art thyself, though not a Montague.
40 What's Montague? It is nor hand nor foot,
Nor arm nor face, nor any other part
Belonging to a man. O be some other name!
What's in a name? That which we call a rose
By any other word would smell as sweet;
45 So Romeo would, were he not Romeo call'd,
Retain that dear perfection which he owes
Without that title. Romeo, doff thy name,
And for thy name, which is no part of thee,
Take all myself.
   **Romeo**
              I take thee at thy word:
50 Call me but love, and I'll be new baptis'd;
Henceforth I never will be Romeo.
   **Juliet**
What man art thou that thus bescreen'd in night
So stumblest on my counsel?
   **Romeo**
                   By a name
I know not how to tell thee who I am.
55 My name, dear saint, is hateful to myself,
Because it is an enemy to thee;
Had I it written, I would tear the word.
   **Juliet**
My ears have yet not drunk a hundred words
Of thy tongue's uttering, yet I know the sound.
60 Art thou not Romeo, and a Montague?
   **Romeo**
Neither, fair maid, if either thee dislike.
   **Juliet**
How cam'st thou hither, tell me, and wherefore?
The orchard walls are high and hard to climb,
And the place death, considering who thou art,
65 If any of my kinsmen find thee here.

---

39 *Thou . . . Montague*: you are yourself (i.e. the man I love) even if you are a Montague.

46 *owes*: owns, possesses.
47 *doff*: cast aside.
48 *for*: in return for.

49 *take . . . word*: accept your promise.

52 *bescreen'd*: concealed, hidden.
53 *counsel*: private meditation.

55 *saint*: Romeo reminds Juliet of their earlier conversation (*1*, 5, 102).

61 *thee dislike*: displeases you.

66 *o'erperch*: fly over.
67 *limits*: boundaries, confines.

69 *stop*: hindrance, obstacle.

72 *Look . . . sweet*: if only you will look
on me with kindness.
73 *proof*: armed.

76 *but*: unless.

78 *prorogued*: proroguèd; postponed,
deferred.
*wanting*: lacking.

82 *pilot*: navigator.
83 *that . . . sea*: the widest shore beyond
the farthest sea.
84 *adventure*: set out as a merchant
tradesman.

86 *maiden blush*: the blush of a virgin.

88 *Fain would I*: I would gladly.
*dwell on form*: observe the rules of
decorum.
89 *compliment*: conventional courtesy.

92 *perjuries*: broken vows.
93 *Jove*: Jupiter, king of the classical
gods.
96 *say thee nay*: (pretend to) refuse you.
97 *So . . . woo*: provided that you
continue to court me.
*else*: otherwise.

**Romeo**
With love's light wings did I o'erperch these walls,
For stony limits cannot hold love out,
And what love can do, that dares love attempt:
Therefore thy kinsmen are no stop to me.
**Juliet**
70 If they do see thee, they will murder thee.
**Romeo**
Alack, there lies more peril in thine eye
Than twenty of their swords. Look thou but sweet,
And I am proof against their enmity.
**Juliet**
I would not for the world they saw thee here.
**Romeo**
75 I have night's cloak to hide me from their eyes,
And but thou love me, let them find me here;
My life were better ended by their hate,
Than death prorogued, wanting of thy love.
**Juliet**
By whose direction found'st thou out this place?
**Romeo**
80 By Love, that first did prompt me to enquire:
He lent me counsel, and I lent him eyes.
I am no pilot, yet wert thou as far
As that vast shore wash'd with the farthest sea,
I should adventure for such merchandise.
**Juliet**
85 Thou knowest the mask of night is on my face,
Else would a maiden blush bepaint my cheek
For that which thou hast heard me speak tonight.
Fain would I dwell on form, fain, fain deny
What I have spoke, but farewell compliment.
90 Dost thou love me? I know thou wilt say 'Ay';
And I will take thy word; yet if thou swear'st,
Thou mayst prove false: at lovers' perjuries
They say Jove laughs. O gentle Romeo,
If thou dost love, pronounce it faithfully;
95 Or if thou think'st I am too quickly won,
I'll frown and be perverse, and say thee nay,
So thou wilt woo, but else not for the world.

98  *fond*: doting, tender-hearted.

99  *light*: immodest.

101  *have . . . strange*: have more
sophistication and can pretend to be
unaffected.
102  *strange*: reserved.
103  *ware*: aware.
104  *true-love*: faithful and loving.

106  *discovered*: discoverèd; revealed.

107  *blessed*: blessèd.

109  *inconstant moon*: The moon, because
of its changes, was a popular emblem
of inconstancy.
110  *circl'd orb*: the sphere in which the
moon circles the earth (according to
Ptolemaic astronomy).

116  *joy in thee*: rejoice in you.
117  *contract*: agreement.

In truth, fair Montague, I am too fond,
And therefore thou mayst think my behaviour light:
100  But trust me, gentleman, I'll prove more true
Than those that have more coying to be strange.
I should have been more strange, I must confess,
But that thou overheard'st, ere I was ware,
My true-love passion; therefore pardon me,
105  And not impute this yielding to light love,
Which the dark night hath so discovered.
    **Romeo**
Lady, by yonder blessed moon I vow,
That tips with silver all these fruit-tree tops—
    **Juliet**
O swear not by the moon, th'inconstant moon,
110  That monthly changes in her circl'd orb,
Lest that thy love prove likewise variable.
    **Romeo**
What shall I swear by?
    **Juliet**
                              Do not swear at all;
Or if thou wilt, swear by thy gracious self,
Which is the god of my idolatry,
115  And I'll believe thee.
    **Romeo**
                              If my heart's dear love—
    **Juliet**
Well, do not swear. Although I joy in thee,
I have no joy of this contract tonight,
It is too rash, too unadvis'd, too sudden,
Too like the lightning, which doth cease to be
120  Ere one can say 'It lightens'. Sweet, good night:
This bud of love, by summer's ripening breath,
May prove a beauteous flower when next we meet.
Good night, good night! as sweet repose and rest
Come to thy heart as that within my breast.
    **Romeo**
125  O wilt thou leave me so unsatisfied?
    **Juliet**
What satisfaction canst thou have tonight?
    **Romeo**
Th'exchange of thy love's faithful vow for mine.

**Juliet**
I gave thee mine before thou didst request it;
And yet I would it were to give again.

**Romeo**
130  Wouldst thou withdraw it? for what purpose, love?

**Juliet**
But to be frank and give it thee again,
And yet I wish but for the thing I have:
My bounty is as boundless as the sea,
My love as deep; the more I give to thee
135  The more I have, for both are infinite.

*Nurse calls within*

I hear some noise within; dear love, adieu!—
Anon, good Nurse!—Sweet Montague, be true.
Stay but a little, I will come again.          [*Exit above*

**Romeo**
O blessed, blessed night! I am afeard,
140  Being in night, all this is but a dream,
Too flattering-sweet to be substantial.

*Enter Juliet above*

**Juliet**
Three words, dear Romeo, and good night indeed.
If that thy bent of love be honourable,
Thy purpose marriage, send me word tomorrow,
145  By one that I'll procure to come to thee,
Where and what time thou wilt perform the rite,
And all my fortunes at thy foot I'll lay,
And follow thee my lord throughout the world.

**Nurse**
[*Within*] Madam!

**Juliet**
150  I come, anon.—But if thou meanest not well,
I do beseech thee—

**Nurse**
[*Within*]                    Madam!

---

129  *I would*: I wish.

131  *frank*: generous.

137  *Anon*: I'm coming.

139  *blessed*: blessèd.

141  *flattering-sweet*: delightfully
attractive.
*substantial*: real.

143  *bent*: intention.

146  *rite*: ceremony.

148  *follow . . . lord*: follow you as my lord.

151 *By and by*: immediately.
152 *strife*: endeavour.

153 *So . . . soul*: as I hope for my soul to be saved.

**Juliet**
                                    By and by I come—
To cease thy strife, and leave me to my grief.
Tomorrow will I send.
      **Romeo**
So thrive my soul—
      **Juliet**
                              A thousand times good night!
                                    [*Exit above*
      **Romeo**
155 A thousand times the worse, to want thy light.
Love goes toward love as schoolboys from their books,
But love from love, toward school with heavy looks.

*Retiring slowly*

*Enter* Juliet *again above*

      **Juliet**
Hist, Romeo, hist! O for a falc'ner's voice,
To lure this tassel-gentle back again:
160 Bondage is hoarse, and may not speak aloud,
Else would I tear the cave where Echo lies,
And make her airy tongue more hoarse than mine
With repetition of my Romeo's name.
      **Romeo**
It is my soul that calls upon my name.
165 How silver-sweet sound lovers' tongues by night,
Like softest music to attending ears!
      **Juliet**
Romeo!
      **Romeo**
      My niësse?
      **Juliet**
                        What a'clock tomorrow
Shall I send to thee?
      **Romeo**
                              By the hour of nine.
      **Juliet**
I will not fail, 'tis twenty year till then.
170 I have forgot why I did call thee back.

158–9 *O for . . . again*: Juliet wishes she could call Romeo back in the way a falconer calls his hawk to pick up the 'lure' (= a bundle of feathers baited with raw flesh).
159 *tassel-gentle*: tercel-gentle, a male hawk.

160 *Bondage is hoarse*: Juliet, bound by the dangers of her situation, cannot raise her voice.
161 *Else*: otherwise.
    *the cave . . . lies*: Echo, a nymph who could only repeat the tag ends of what she heard others say, fell in love with Narcissus; when he rejected her, she retreated to an empty cave.
162 *airy*: disembodied.
167 *niësse*: young unfledged hawk, nestling hawk.

**Romeo**
Let me stand here till thou remember it.
   **Juliet**
I shall forget, to have thee still stand there,
Rememb'ring how I love thy company.
   **Romeo**
And I'll still stay, to have thee still forget,
175 Forgetting any other home but this.
   **Juliet**
'Tis almost morning, I would have thee gone:
And yet no farther than a wanton's bird,
That lets it hop a little from his hand,
Like a poor prisoner in his twisted gyves,
180 And with a silken thread plucks it back again,
So loving-jealous of his liberty.
   **Romeo**
I would I were thy bird.
   **Juliet**
                Sweet, so would I,
Yet I should kill thee with much cherishing.
Good night, good night! Parting is such sweet sorrow,
185 That I shall say good night till it be morrow.
                              *[Exit above*

   **Romeo**
Sleep dwell upon thine eyes, peace in thy breast!
Would I were sleep and peace, so sweet to rest!
Hence will I to my ghostly sire's close cell,
His help to crave, and my dear hap to tell.    *[Exit*

## Scene 3

*Monday morning*: Friar Lawrence's cell. Enter Friar
Lawrence *alone, with a basket*

   **Friar Lawrence**
The grey-ey'd morn smiles on the frowning night,
Check'ring the eastern clouds with streaks of light;
And fleckled darkness like a drunkard reels
From forth day's path and Titan's fiery wheels:
5 Now ere the sun advance his burning eye,
The day to cheer, and night's dank dew to dry,

177 *wanton's*: pampered child's.

179 *gyves*: shackles.
188 *ghostly sire's*: spiritual father's.
    *close*: secluded.
189 *dear hap*: good fortune.

**Act 2 Scene 3**
Friar Lawrence is persuaded to marry
Romeo and Juliet.

3 *fleckled*: dappled with streaks of red
  (like a drunkard's face).
4 *From forth*: out of the way of.
  *Titan's fiery wheels*: the burning
  wheels of the chariot of the sun-god,
  the Titan Helios.

7 *osier cage*: willow basket.
*ours*: i.e. belonging to the religious
order, and not his own possession.
8 *baleful*: harmful, poisonous.
*juiced*: juicèd.

11 *divers*: various.

12 *sucking on*: receiving nourishment
from.

14 *None . . . some*: all of them have
some good qualities.
15 *mickle*: great.
*grace*: healing virtue.

19 *strain'd*: forced, perverted.

20 *true birth*: its proper nature.
*stumbling on abuse*: finding some
harmful application.
22 *vice . . . dignified*: evil sometimes
made good by the right action.

23 *infant*: undeveloped.
24 *Poison . . . power*: there resides both
poison and the healing power of
medicine.
25 *that part*: i.e. its scent.
26 *stays . . . heart*: arrests all senses by
stopping the heart.
27 *opposed*: opposèd.
*still*: always.
28 *grace . . . will*: divine virtue and
unruly (human) desire.
30 *canker*: canker-worm (which devours
the flower from inside); compare
*1, 1, 145*.

I must upfill this osier cage of ours
With baleful weeds and precious-juiced flowers.
The earth that's nature's mother is her tomb;
10 What is her burying grave, that is her womb;
And from her womb children of divers kind
We sucking on her natural bosom find:
Many for many virtues excellent,
None but for some, and yet all different.
15 O mickle is the powerful grace that lies
In plants, herbs, stones, and their true qualities:
For nought so vile, that on the earth doth live,
But to the earth some special good doth give;
Nor ought so good but, strain'd from that fair use,
20 Revolts from true birth, stumbling on abuse.
Virtue itself turns vice, being misapplied,
And vice sometime by action dignified.

*Enter* Romeo

Within the infant rind of this weak flower
Poison hath residence, and medicine power:
25 For this, being smelt, with that part cheers each part,
Being tasted, stays all senses with the heart.
Two such opposed kings encamp them still
In man as well as herbs, grace and rude will;
And where the worser is predominant,
30 Full soon the canker death eats up that plant.
   **Romeo**
Good morrow, father.

**Friar Lawrence**

Benedicite!

What early tongue so sweet saluteth me?

Young son, it argues a distemper'd head

So soon to bid good morrow to thy bed:

35 Care keeps his watch in every old man's eye,

And where care lodges, sleep will never lie;

But where unbruised youth with unstuff'd brain

Doth couch his limbs, there golden sleep doth reign.

Therefore thy earliness doth me assure

40 Thou art uprous'd with some distemp'rature;

Or if not so, then here I hit it right,

Our Romeo hath not been in bed tonight.

**Romeo**

That last is true, the sweeter rest was mine.

**Friar Lawrence**

God pardon sin! wast thou with Rosaline?

**Romeo**

45 With Rosaline, my ghostly father? no;

I have forgot that name, and that name's woe.

**Friar Lawrence**

That's my good son, but where hast thou been then?

**Romeo**

I'll tell thee ere thou ask it me again:

I have been feasting with mine enemy,

50 Where on a sudden one hath wounded me

That's by me wounded; both our remedies

Within thy help and holy physic lies.

I bear no hatred, blessed man; for lo,

My intercession likewise steads my foe.

**Friar Lawrence**

55 Be plain, good son, and homely in thy drift,

Riddling confession finds but riddling shrift.

**Romeo**

Then plainly know, my heart's dear love is set

On the fair daughter of rich Capulet;

As mine on hers, so hers is set on mine,

60 And all combin'd, save what thou must combine

By holy marriage. When and where and how

We met, we woo'd, and made exchange of vow,

I'll tell thee as we pass, but this I pray,

That thou consent to marry us today.

---

31 *Benedicite*: God bless you.

33 *argues*: suggests.
*distemper'd*: disturbed.
34 *bid . . . to*: say goodbye to, get up from.

37 *unbruised*: unbruisèd; unharmed (by experience).
*unstuff'd*: untroubled.
38 *couch*: rest.

41 *hit*: guess.

45 *ghostly*: spiritual.
46 *that name's woe*: the misery I suffered because of the name 'Rosaline'.

51 *both our remedies*: cures for both of us.

53 *blessed*: blessèd.
54 *intercession*: prayer, petition.
*steads*: benefits.

55 *homely*: simple.
*thy drift*: what you say.
56 *Riddling*: ambiguous, difficult to understand.
*shrift*: absolution.
57 *plainly*: simply.

63 *pass*: go along.

**Friar Lawrence**

65 Holy Saint Francis, what a change is here!
Is Rosaline, that thou didst love so dear,
So soon forsaken? Young men's love then lies
Not truly in their hearts, but in their eyes.
Jesu Maria, what a deal of brine
70 Hath wash'd thy sallow cheeks for Rosaline!
How much salt water thrown away in waste,
To season love, that of it doth not taste!
The sun not yet thy sighs from heaven clears,
Thy old groans yet ringing in mine ancient ears;
75 Lo here upon thy cheek the stain doth sit
Of an old tear that is not wash'd off yet.
If e'er thou wast thyself, and these woes thine,
Thou and these woes were all for Rosaline.
And art thou chang'd? Pronounce this sentence then:
80 Women may fall, when there's no strength in men.

**Romeo**

Thou chid'st me oft for loving Rosaline.

**Friar Lawrence**

For doting, not for loving, pupil mine.

**Romeo**

And bad'st me bury love.

**Friar Lawrence**

                                   Not in a grave,
To lay one in, another out to have.

**Romeo**

85 I pray thee chide me not. Her I love now
Doth grace for grace and love for love allow;
The other did not so.

**Friar Lawrence**

                                O she knew well
Thy love did read by rote, that could not spell.
But come, young waverer, come go with me,
90 In one respect I'll thy assistant be:
For this alliance may so happy prove
To turn your households' rancour to pure love.

**Romeo**

O let us hence, I stand on sudden haste.

**Friar Lawrence**

Wisely and slow, they stumble that run fast. [*Exeunt*

69 *Jesu Maria*: by Jesus and Mary.
   *a deal of brine*: a lot of salt water.
70 *sallow*: sickly, pale (from unrequited love).
72 *To season . . . taste*: in hope of improving hopeless love that you now no longer enjoy.

77 *wast thyself*: were sincere.

79 *sentence*: moral maxim, wise saying.
80 *may fall*: can be excused for falling.

81 *chid'st*: scolded.

86 *grace*: favour.
   *allow*: return.

88 *Thy love . . . spell*: you had learned the words by heart without understanding them.
90 *In one respect*: for a special reason.

93 *stand on*: insist on.

Benvolio and Mercutio discuss Tybalt's
challenge, and Romeo joins in their
laughter—until Juliet's Nurse comes to find
him.

1 *should*: can.

2 *tonight*: last night.

9 *answer it*: accept the challenge.
11–12 *how . . . dared*: as much as he
dares, having been challenged.
14 *run*: pierced.
15 *the very pin*: the pin marking the
centre of the target.
15–16 *blind bow-boy*: Cupid.
16 *butt-shaft*: the thick end of his arrow.
19 *Prince of Cats*: Tibault, a cat in a
Dutch fable, was described as 'Prince
of Cats' by Thomas Nashe,
Shakespeare's contemporary.
20 *captain of compliments*: expert in the
art of duelling (i.e. in the latest Italian
style).
20–1 *prick-song*: printed music (sung
with greater accuracy than
remembered tunes).
21 *time*: rhythm.
*distance, and proportion*: the correct
distance, and proper bodily
movement, between the opponents;
tempo and properly observed intervals
in music.
21–2 *he rests . . . bosom*: he makes two
feints with the briefest of pauses
between them, and strikes to the heart
on the third beat; a 'minim' is the
shortest note in music.
23 *butcher . . . button*: An expert duellist
could slice through his opponent's
buttons.
24 *house*: school of fencing.
24–5 *first . . . cause*: Only two causes
were recognized as acceptable for a
duel: (a) being accused of major
crime; (b) personal or family honour.
Tybalt challenges Romeo on the
second cause.

# SCENE 4

*Verona: a street. Enter* Benvolio *and* Mercutio

**Mercutio**
Where the dev'l should this Romeo be?
Came he not home tonight?
**Benvolio**
Not to his father's, I spoke with his man.
**Mercutio**
Why, that same pale hard-hearted wench, that
Rosaline,
5 Torments him so, that he will sure run mad.
**Benvolio**
Tybalt, the kinsman to old Capulet,
Hath sent a letter to his father's house.
**Mercutio**
A challenge, on my life.
**Benvolio**
Romeo will answer it.
**Mercutio**
10 Any man that can write may answer a letter.
**Benvolio**
Nay, he will answer the letter's master, how he dares,
being dared.
**Mercutio**
Alas, poor Romeo, he is already dead, stabbed with a
white wench's black eye, run through the ear with a
15 love-song, the very pin of his heart cleft with the blind
bow-boy's butt-shaft; and is he a man to encounter
Tybalt?
**Benvolio**
Why, what is Tybalt?
**Mercutio**
More than Prince of Cats. O, he's the courageous
20 captain of compliments: he fights as you sing prick-
song, keeps time, distance, and proportion; he rests his
minim rests, one, two, and the third in your bosom; the
very butcher of a silk button, a duellist, a duellist; a
gentleman of the very first house, of the first and second

25 *immortal*: famous; death-dealing.
25–6 *'passado . . . hay'*: The latest
    technical terms for duelling: (1) a
    step, and thrust forward; (2) a back-
    handed stroke; (3) a stab to the heart
    (from the Italian '*hai*' = you have it).
28 *pox of*: plague on.
    *antic*: absurd.
    *affecting phantasimes*: would-be
    gallant gentlemen.
29 *new . . . accent*: affected speakers
    with fancy pronunciations.
29–30 *'By Jesu . . . whore'*: Mercutio
    imitates the objects of his scorn.
29 *blade*: sword.
30 *tall*: valiant.
31 *grandsire*: grandfather; Mercutio
    addresses Benvolio as one old man to
    another.
32 *strange flies*: queer (foreign) parasites.
    *fashion-mongers*: followers of the
    latest fashion (in dress and speech).
33 *pardon-me's*: those who are always
    excusing themselves (in a French
    manner).
33–4 *stand . . . bench*: those who insist
    so much on the latest styles that they
    are uncomfortable with the old ways;
    Mercutio plays on 'form' = hard seat.
34–5 *O their bones*: their bones are
    aching from sitting on the 'old
    bench'—or perhaps they have 'bone-
    ache' (syphilis, also called the 'French
    disease').
37–8 *Without . . . fishified*: Mercutio
    implies that Romeo is exhausted after
    spending the night with a prostitute;
    'roe' = a) fish eggs; b) a small deer.
38–9 *for . . . flowed in*: in favour of the
    sonnets that Petrarch (a fourteenth-
    century Italian poet) wrote so easily.
39 *Laura*: Petrarch's mistress.
    *to*: in comparison with.
40 *love*: lover.
    *berhyme*: write verses to her.
41 *Dido a dowdy*: Dido (heroine of
    Christopher Marlowe's play *Dido,
    Queen of Carthage*) was a slovenly,
    nondescript woman.
    *Cleopatra a gipsy*: the Queen of Egypt
    (later the subject of *Antony and
    Cleopatra*) was merely a dusky wench.
    *Helen*: Helen of Troy, said to be the
    most beautiful woman in the world.
    *Hero*: The heroine of Marlowe's
    narrative poem, *Hero and Leander*.

25 cause. Ah, the immortal 'passado', the 'punto reverso',
the 'hay'!
   **Benvolio**
The what?
   **Mercutio**
The pox of such antic, lisping, affecting phantasimes,
these new tuners of accent! 'By Jesu, a very good blade!
30 a very tall man! a very good whore!' Why, is not this a
lamentable thing, grandsire, that we should be thus
afflicted with these strange flies, these fashion-mongers,
these pardon-me's, who stand so much on the new
form, that they cannot sit at ease on the old bench? O
35 their bones, their bones!

   *Enter* Romeo

   **Benvolio**
Here comes Romeo, here comes Romeo.
   **Mercutio**
Without his roe, like a dried herring: O flesh, flesh, how
art thou fishified! Now is he for the numbers that
Petrarch flowed in. Laura to his lady was a kitchen
40 wench (marry, she had a better love to berhyme her),
Dido a dowdy, Cleopatra a gipsy, Helen and Hero

42 *hildings and harlots*: tarts and
   prostitutes.
   *Thisbe*: the heroine of 'Pyramus and
   Thisbe', Shakespeare's parody of
   heroic tragedy in *A Midsummer
   Night's Dream*.
42–3 *not to the purpose*: nothing in
   comparison (with Romeo's lady).
43 *'bon jour'*: good day.
44 *French slop*: loose-fitting, short
   breeches; Romeo still wears his
   masquerade costume.
44–5 *gave . . . counterfeit*: tricked us.
48 *slip*: a slang term for a counterfeit
   coin.
   *conceive*: understand.
49 *great*: important.
49–50 *in such . . . courtesy*: in such a
   contingency a man may forget good
   manners.
51–2 *That's . . . hams*: such a (sexual)
   condition as yours forces a man to go
   weak at the knees.
53 *cur'sy*: make a bow.

54 *kindly hit it*: graciously taken the
   point; naturally made the connection.
56 *pink*: (a) perfect example; (b) a kind
   of flower; (c) to make a pattern of
   holes in leather.
59 *then . . . flowered*: then my dancing-
   shoe is well decorated with flowers.
60 *Follow . . . jest*: follow this joke for my
   sake.
61 *single sole*: thin material of the sole.
62 *solely singular*: valuable in being
   singular.
63 *O single-soled . . . singleness*: a trivial
   joke, which is remarkable ('singular')
   only for being single.
64 *Come . . . us*: stop this punning duel.
65 *Swits and spurs*: use whip and spurs
   (to keep your wits galloping).
   *cry a match*: claim the victory.

hildings and harlots, Thisbe a grey eye or so, but not to
the purpose. Signior Romeo, 'bon jour'! there's a French
salutation to your French slop. You gave us the
45 counterfeit fairly last night.

**Romeo**

Good morrow to you both. What counterfeit did I give
you?

**Mercutio**

The slip, sir, the slip, can you not conceive?

**Romeo**

Pardon, good Mercutio, my business was great, and in
50 such a case as mine a man may strain courtesy.

**Mercutio**

That's as much as to say, such a case as yours constrains
a man to bow in the hams.

**Romeo**

Meaning to cur'sy.

**Mercutio**

Thou hast most kindly hit it.

**Romeo**

55 A most courteous exposition.

**Mercutio**

Nay, I am the very pink of courtesy.

**Romeo**

Pink for flower.

**Mercutio**

Right.

**Romeo**

Why then is my pump well flowered.

**Mercutio**

60 Sure wit! Follow me this jest now, till thou hast worn
out thy pump, that when the single sole of it is worn, the
jest may remain, after the wearing, solely singular.

**Romeo**

O single-soled jest, solely singular for the singleness!

**Mercutio**

Come between us, good Benvolio, my wits faints.

**Romeo**

65 Swits and spurs, swits and spurs, or I'll cry a match.

66 *wild-goose chase*: a race in which the leader chooses his own course.
67 *wild goose*: nitwit, nincompoop.
68 *my whole five*: all my five wits (common-sense, memory, imagination, fancy, and judgement).
68–9 *Was I . . . goose*: did I score a point from you with the word 'goose' (= a) prostitute; b) foolish fellow).

72 *bite . . . ear*: give you an affectionate nibble.

74 *sweeting*: apple (used for making the traditional sauce for roast goose).

75 *served in to*: served with.
76–7 *here's . . . broad*: i.e. you're stretching your little wit as far as it can go; 'cheverel' (= soft, stretchy, kid leather) begins 'ch' and ends 'l'.
77 *ell*: 45 inches (approx. 115 centimetres).
78 *I stretch it out*: I'll make it go even further.
*broad*: (a) wide; (b) obvious; (c) indecent.
79 *a broad goose*: a goose that only hatches others' eggs (i.e. Romeo's own wit).
82 *by art*: by application of skill.
83 *natural*: idiot, fool.
*lolling*: with his tongue hanging out.
84 *bauble*: decorated stick carried by professional jester.
85 *Stop*: Benvolio has heard enough of these bawdy quibbles—but Mercutio takes him in another sense.
86 *stop in*: (a) cease; (b) stuff in.
*tale*: (a) story; (b) penis.
*against the hair*: unnaturally, against my desires.
87 *large*: long; Benvolio joins in the quibbling.
88–9 *I was . . . tale*: (a) I had come to the end of my story; (b) I had achieved orgasm.
90 *occupy*: (a) continue in; (b) have intercourse with.
91 *gear*: (a) rubbish; (b) sexual equipment.

**Mercutio**
Nay, if our wits run the wild-goose chase, I am done; for thou hast more of the wild goose in one of thy wits than, I am sure, I have in my whole five. Was I with you there for the goose?
**Romeo**
70 Thou wast never with me for any thing when thou wast not there for the goose.
**Mercutio**
I will bite thee by the ear for that jest.
**Romeo**
Nay, good goose, bite not.
**Mercutio**
Thy wit is very bitter sweeting, it is a most sharp sauce.
**Romeo**
75 And is it not then well served in to a sweet goose?
**Mercutio**
O here's a wit of cheverel, that stretches from an inch narrow to an ell broad!
**Romeo**
I stretch it out for that word 'broad', which, added to the goose, proves thee far and wide a broad goose.
**Mercutio**
80 Why, is not this better now than groaning for love? Now art thou sociable, now art thou Romeo; now art thou what thou art, by art as well as by nature, for this drivelling love is like a great natural that runs lolling up and down to hide his bauble in a hole.
**Benvolio**
85 Stop there, stop there.
**Mercutio**
Thou desirest me to stop in my tale against the hair.
**Benvolio**
Thou wouldst else have made thy tale large.
**Mercutio**
O thou art deceived; I would have made it short, for I was come to the whole depth of my tale, and meant
90 indeed to occupy the argument no longer.
**Romeo**
Here's goodly gear!

*Enter* Nurse *and her man* Peter

92 *A sail, a sail*: Romeo sees the Nurse coming towards them like a ship on the horizon.

93 *a shirt . . . smock*: a man and a woman.
95 *Anon*: immediately, I'm coming.
98 *God . . . morrow*: may God give you a good morning.
99 *good den*: good even (i.e. afternoon).

101 *dial*: sundial, clock-face; woman.
102 *prick*: point; penis.

103 *Out . . . are you*: get away with you! What kind of man are you.

105 *mar*: spoil.

106 *By my troth*: upon my word, by my faith.
    *quoth'a*: says he, indeed.

111 *fault*: lack.

113 *took*: understood—though in fact the Nurse has understood nothing.

A sail, a sail!
**Mercutio**
Two, two: a shirt and a smock.
**Nurse**
Peter!
**Peter**
95 Anon.
**Nurse**
My fan, Peter.
**Mercutio**
Good Peter, to hide her face, for her fan's the fairer face.
**Nurse**
God ye good morrow, gentlemen.
**Mercutio**
God ye good den, fair gentlewoman.
**Nurse**
100 Is it good den?
**Mercutio**
'Tis no less, I tell ye, for the bawdy hand of the dial is now upon the prick of noon.
**Nurse**
Out upon you, what a man are you?
**Romeo**
One, gentlewoman, that God hath made, himself to
105 mar.
**Nurse**
By my troth, it is well said: 'for himself to mar', quoth'a? Gentlemen, can any of you tell me where I may find the young Romeo?
**Romeo**
I can tell you, but young Romeo will be older when you
110 have found him than he was when you sought him: I am the youngest of that name, for fault of a worse.
**Nurse**
You say well.
**Mercutio**
Yea, is the worst well? Very well took, i'faith, wisely, wisely.

115 *confidence*: The Nurse's malapropism (misapplied word) for 'conference' (= talk).
116 *indite*: invite; Benvolio imitates the Nurse with another malapropism.
117 *bawd*: (a) brothel-keeper, procurer; (b) hare (in North-Midland dialect). *So ho!*: The cry of a hunter when he sees his quarry.

119 *a hare . . . pie*: the sort of hare you would find in a pie for eating during Lent (a time of fasting).
120 *hoar*: mouldy (with a pun on 'whore'). *spent*: finished.

125 *too . . . score*: not worth putting on the bill.
126 *hoars*: (a) goes mouldy; (b) becomes a whore.
127 *dinner*: This was eaten about midday.

130 *Farewell . . . farewell*: Mercutio sings the refrain of a popular song.

133 *ropery*: roguery, knavery.

135 *speak*: promise. *stand to*: perform.
137 *And 'a speak*: if he speaks. *take him down*: lower his pride.
138 *Jacks*: ill-mannered fellows, knaves.
140 *flirt-gills*: loose women. *skains-mates*: fighting companions ('skains' = long Irish daggers).
142 *suffer*: allow. *use . . . pleasure*: treat me as he pleased; Peter's response gives a bawdy twist to these words.

**Nurse**
115 If you be he, sir, I desire some confidence with you.
  **Benvolio**
She will indite him to some supper.
  **Mercutio**
A bawd, a bawd, a bawd! So ho!
  **Romeo**
What hast thou found?
  **Mercutio**
No hare, sir, unless a hare, sir, in a lenten pie, that is
120 something stale and hoar ere it be spent.

*He walks by them and sings*

> An old hare hoar,
> And an old hare hoar,
> Is very good meat in Lent;
> But a hare that is hoar
125 Is too much for a score,
> When it hoars ere it be spent.

Romeo, will you come to your father's? We'll to dinner
thither.
  **Romeo**
I will follow you.
  **Mercutio**
130 Farewell, ancient lady, farewell, lady, [*Singing*] 'lady,
lady'.                         [*Exeunt* Mercutio *and* Benvolio
  **Nurse**
I pray you, sir, what saucy merchant was this that was so
full of his ropery?
  **Romeo**
A gentleman, Nurse, that loves to hear himself talk, and
135 will speak more in a minute than he will stand to in a
month.
  **Nurse**
And 'a speak any thing against me, I'll take him down,
and 'a were lustier than he is, and twenty such Jacks; and
if I cannot, I'll find those that shall. Scurvy knave, I am
140 none of his flirt-gills, I am none of his skains-mates.
[*She turns to* Peter, *her man*] And thou must stand by
too and suffer every knave to use me at his pleasure!

**Peter**

I saw no man use you at his pleasure; if I had, my
weapon should quickly have been out. I warrant you, I
145   dare draw as soon as another man, if I see occasion in a
good quarrel, and the law on my side.

**Nurse**

Now afore God, I am so vexed that every part about me
quivers. Scurvy knave! Pray you, sir, a word: and as I
told you, my young lady bid me enquire you out; what
150   she bid me say, I will keep to myself. But first let me tell
ye, if ye should lead her in a fool's paradise, as they say,
it were a very gross kind of behaviour, as they say; for
the gentlewoman is young; and therefore, if you should
deal double with her, truly it were an ill thing to be
155   offered to any gentlewoman, and very weak dealing.

**Romeo**

Nurse, commend me to thy lady and mistress. I protest
unto thee—

**Nurse**

Good heart, and i'faith I will tell her as much. Lord,
Lord, she will be a joyful woman.

**Romeo**

160   What wilt thou tell her, Nurse? thou dost not mark me.

**Nurse**

I will tell her, sir, that you do protest, which, as I take it,
is a gentleman-like offer.

**Romeo**

Bid her devise
Some means to come to shrift this afternoon,
165   And there she shall at Friar Lawrence' cell
Be shriv'd and married. Here is for thy pains.

**Nurse**

No truly, sir, not a penny.

**Romeo**

Go to, I say you shall.

**Nurse**

This afternoon, sir? Well, she shall be there.

**Romeo**

170   And stay, good Nurse, behind the abbey wall:
Within this hour my man shall be with thee,
And bring thee cords made like a tackl'd stair,

---

151  *lead . . . paradise*: i.e. seduce her.

154  *deal double*: deceive.
155  *weak dealing*: shameful conduct.

156  *commend me*: convey my best wishes.
    *protest*: solemnly promise, vow.

160  *mark me*: pay attention to what I am
    saying.

164  *shrift*: confession.

166  *shriv'd*: given absolution after
    confession; this was essential for
    receiving the sacrament of marriage.
    *pains*: trouble; Romeo offers money to
    the Nurse.

172  *cords*: ropes.
    *tackl'd stair*: rope ladder.

173 *top-gallant*: the platform at the head of a ship's mast.
174 *convoy*: means of access.
175 *quit*: requite, reward.

179 *secret*: trustworthy.

180 *Two . . . away*: two people can keep a secret when one of them (or a third person) is away.
181 *'Warrant*: I warrant.

183 *prating*: prattling, chattering.

184–5 *would . . . aboard*: would very much like to assert his claim; diners reserved their places by setting their own knives on the table ('board').
185 *had as lieve*: would as willingly.
186 *sometimes*: The speed of the play's action allows the Nurse very little time for such teasing!
187 *the properer*: the more handsome.
188 *clout*: washed-out rag.
     *versal*: universal, whole.
189 *rosemary*: the herb of remembrance, worn at weddings and funerals.
189–90 *both with a letter*: with the same letter (the nurse is illiterate).
192 *dog-name*: A Roman poet, Persius, called 'R' the dog-letter because it sounded like the growl of a dog.
192–3 *'R' is . . . letter*: The Nurse is about to say 'arse', but decides that this is rude and there must be another initial letter for 'Romeo' and 'rosemary'.
194 *sententious*: The Nurse means 'sentence' (= proverb, witty saying).

199 *apace*: quickly.

Which to the high top-gallant of my joy
Must be my convoy in the secret night.
175 Farewell, be trusty, and I'll quit thy pains.
Farewell, commend me to thy mistress.

**Nurse**
Now God in heaven bless thee! Hark you, sir.

**Romeo**
What say'st thou, my dear Nurse?

**Nurse**
Is your man secret? Did you ne'er hear say,
180 'Two may keep counsel, putting one away'?

**Romeo**
'Warrant thee, my man's as true as steel.

**Nurse**
Well, sir, my mistress is the sweetest lady—Lord, Lord!
when 'twas a little prating thing—O, there is a
nobleman in town, one Paris, that would fain lay knife
185 aboard; but she, good soul, had as lieve see a toad, a very
toad, as see him. I anger her sometimes, and tell her that
Paris is the properer man, but I'll warrant you, when I
say so, she looks as pale as any clout in the versal world.
Doth not rosemary and Romeo begin both with
190 a letter?

**Romeo**
Ay, Nurse, what of that? Both with an R.

**Nurse**
Ah, mocker, that's the dog-name. R is for the—no, I
know it begins with some other letter—and she hath
the prettiest sententious of it, of you and rosemary, that
195 it would do you good to hear it.

**Romeo**
Commend me to thy lady.

**Nurse**
Ay, a thousand times.                                    [*Exit* Romeo
                         Peter!

**Peter**
Anon.

**Nurse**
[*Handing him her fan*] Before and apace.
                                              [*Exit after* Peter

**Act 2 Scene 5**
The Nurse tells Juliet about Romeo's
arrangements for their marriage.

3 *Perchance*: perhaps.

6 *low'ring*: gloomy.
7 *Therefore . . . Love*: for that reason
the chariot of Venus (goddess of love)
is drawn by swift-winged doves.
9 *upon . . . hill*: at the meridian, at its
height.

12 *affections*: desires.

14 *bandy her*: strike her like a tennis ball.

16 *many . . . dead*: a lot of them act as
though they were already dead.

22 *them*: the news (the noun could be
treated as either singular or plural).

26 *jaunce*: uncomfortable jolting trip.

# Scene 5

Capulet's *house: enter* Juliet

**Juliet**
The clock struck nine when I did send the Nurse;
In half an hour she promis'd to return.
Perchance she cannot meet him: that's not so.
O, she is lame! Love's heralds should be thoughts,
5 Which ten times faster glides than the sun's beams,
Driving back shadows over low'ring hills;
Therefore do nimble-pinion'd doves draw Love,
And therefore hath the wind-swift Cupid wings.
Now is the sun upon the highmost hill
10 Of this day's journey, and from nine till twelve
Is three long hours, yet she is not come.
Had she affections and warm youthful blood,
She would be as swift in motion as a ball;
My words would bandy her to my sweet love,
15 And his to me.
But old folks, many feign as they were dead,
Unwieldy, slow, heavy, and pale as lead.

*Enter* Nurse *with* Peter

O God, she comes! O honey Nurse, what news?
Hast thou met with him? Send thy man away.
**Nurse**
20 Peter, stay at the gate.                    [*Exit* Peter
**Juliet**
Now, good sweet Nurse—O Lord, why look'st thou sad?
Though news be sad, yet tell them merrily;
If good, thou shamest the music of sweet news
By playing it to me with so sour a face.
**Nurse**
25 I am a-weary, give me leave a while.
Fie, how my bones ache! What a jaunce have I!
**Juliet**
I would thou hadst my bones, and I thy news.
Nay, come, I pray thee speak, good, good Nurse, speak.

29 *stay a while*: wait a moment.

33 *in this delay*: for this delay.

36 *stay the circumstance*: wait for the
details.

38 *simple*: foolish.

41–2 *not to be talked on*: not worth
talking about.

43 *flower*: model.

44 *Go . . . God*: enough of this, my girl,
behave yourself.

50 *a't'other side*: on the other side.

51 *Beshrew*: curse.

52 *jauncing*: tripping.

55 *honest*: honourable.

**Nurse**
Jesu, what haste! can you not stay a while?
30 Do you not see that I am out of breath?
**Juliet**
How art thou out of breath, when thou hast breath
To say to me that thou art out of breath?
The excuse that thou dost make in this delay
Is longer than the tale thou dost excuse.
35 Is thy news good or bad? Answer to that.
Say either, and I'll stay the circumstance:
Let me be satisfied, is't good or bad?
**Nurse**
Well, you have made a simple choice, you know not how
to choose a man: Romeo? no, not he; though his face be
40 better than any man's, yet his leg excels all men's, and for
a hand and a foot and a body, though they be not to be
talked on, yet they are past compare. He is not the
flower of courtesy, but I'll warrant him, as gentle as a
lamb. Go thy ways, wench, serve God. What, have you
45 dined at home?
**Juliet**
No, no! But all this did I know before.
What says he of our marriage, what of that?
**Nurse**
Lord, how my head aches! what a head have I!
It beats as it would fall in twenty pieces.
50 My back a't'other side—ah, my back, my back!
Beshrew your heart for sending me about
To catch my death with jauncing up and down!
**Juliet**
I'faith, I am sorry that thou art not well.
Sweet, sweet, sweet Nurse, tell me, what says my love?
**Nurse**
55 Your love says, like an honest gentleman,
And a courteous, and a kind, and a handsome,
And I warrant a virtuous—Where is your mother?
**Juliet**
Where is my mother? why, she is within,
Where should she be? How oddly thou repliest:
60 'Your love says, like an honest gentleman,
"Where is your mother?"'

**Nurse**

O God's lady dear,

61 *God's lady*: the Virgin Mary.

62 *hot*: impatient.

Are you so hot? Marry come up, I trow;
Is this the poultice for my aching bones?
Henceforward do your messages yourself.

**Juliet**

65 *coil*: fuss.

65 Here's such a coil! Come, what says Romeo?

**Nurse**

66 *shrift*: confession.

Have you got leave to go to shrift today?

**Juliet**

I have.

**Nurse**

68 *hie*: go.

Then hie you hence to Friar Lawrence' cell,
There stays a husband to make you a wife.

70 *wanton*: uncontrolled.

71 *be in scarlet*: blush.

70 Now comes the wanton blood up in your cheeks,
They'll be in scarlet straight at any news.
Hie you to church, I must another way,
To fetch a ladder, by the which your love
Must climb a bird's nest soon when it is dark.

75 *toil in your delight*: labour for your happiness.
76 *bear the burden*: carry (a) the responsibility; (b) the weight of your lover.

75 I am the drudge, and toil in your delight;
But you shall bear the burden soon at night.
Go, I'll to dinner, hie you to the cell.

**Juliet**

Hie to high fortune! Honest Nurse, farewell.　　*[Exeunt*

'Hie you hence to Friar Lawrence' cell', (*2*, 5, 68). Margaret Courtenay as Nurse and Georgia Slowe as Juliet, Royal Shakespeare Company, 1989.

**Act 2 Scene 6**
Romeo and Juliet are married.

## SCENE 6

*Friar Lawrence's cell: enter* Friar Lawrence *and* Romeo

**Friar Lawrence**
So smile the heavens upon this holy act,
That after-hours with sorrow chide us not.
   **Romeo**
Amen, amen! but come what sorrow can,
It cannot countervail the exchange of joy
5 That one short minute gives me in her sight.
Do thou but close our hands with holy words,
Then love-devouring Death do what he dare,
It is enough I may but call her mine.
   **Friar Lawrence**
These violent delights have violent ends,
10 And in their triumph die like fire and powder,
Which as they kiss consume. The sweetest honey
Is loathsome in his own deliciousness,
And in the taste confounds the appetite.
Therefore love moderately, long love doth so;
15 Too swift arrives as tardy as too slow.

*Enter* Juliet

Here comes the lady. O, so light a foot
Will ne'er wear out the everlasting flint;
A lover may bestride the gossamers
That idles in the wanton summer air,
20 And yet not fall, so light is vanity.
   **Juliet**
Good even to my ghostly confessor.
   **Friar Lawrence**
Romeo shall thank thee, daughter, for us both.

*Romeo kisses* Juliet

1–2 *So smile . . . not*: may the heavens look favourably upon this holy action, so that times to come ('after-hours') do not bring sorrow to reproach us.
3–5 *come . . . sight*: whatever sorrow may come, it will not equal ('countervail') the delight that I receive in exchange from one short minute in Juliet's sight.
6 *Do . . . hands*: all you have to do is join our hands.
8 *but*: only.

10 *powder*: gun-powder.

12 *his*: its.
13 *in . . . appetite*: ruins the appetite in tasting it.

15 *tardy*: late.

16–20 *O, so light . . . fall*: Even the Friar seems to be susceptible to Juliet's charms.
17 *everlasting flint*: hard-wearing cobbles (that she treads upon).
18 *bestride*: ride upon.
*gossamers*: spiders' webs.
19 *idles*: floats.
*wanton*: playful.
20 *vanity*: the insubstantiality of worldly pleasures; the Friar remembers his profession ('Vanity of vanities, saith the Preacher, vanity of vanities, all is vanity', Ecclesiastes 1:2).
21 *ghostly confessor*: spiritual father; 'confessor' is stressed on the first syllable.

**Juliet**
As much to him, else is his thanks too much.

*Juliet returns his kiss*

**Romeo**
Ah, Juliet, if the measure of thy joy
25 Be heap'd like mine, and that thy skill be more
To blazon it, then sweeten with thy breath
This neighbour air, and let rich music's tongue
Unfold the imagin'd happiness that both
Receive in either by this dear encounter.
**Juliet**
30 Conceit, more rich in matter than in words,
Brags of his substance, not of ornament;
They are but beggars that can count their worth,
But my true love is grown to such excess
I cannot sum up sum of half my wealth.
**Friar Lawrence**
35 Come, come with me, and we will make short work,
For by your leaves, you shall not stay alone
Till Holy Church incorporate two in one.        [*Exeunt*

23 *As much . . . too much*: I must return his kiss, or else I shall be overpaid.

24 *measure*: measuring-cup.

26 *blazon*: describe (a heraldic term).

27 *neighbour*: surrounding.
*rich music's tongue*: the musical harmony of your words.
28 *Unfold*: express.
29 *in either*: in each other.

30 *Conceit*: imagination.
*matter*: substance, the inner reality.
31 *Brags . . . ornament*: takes pride in that substance.
32 *They . . . worth*: only beggars can tell you how much money they have.
34 *sum up sum*: add up the total amount.

36 *by your leaves*: if you'll excuse me.

'Mercutio, thou consortest with Romeo', (3, 1, 42). Simon Templeman as Tybalt, James Simmons as Benvolio, and Roger Allam as Mercutio, Royal Shakespeare Company, 1983.

**Act 3 Scene 1**
Mercutio, outraged when Romeo refuses
Tybalt's challenge, draws his own sword,
and in the fighting that follows both he and
Tybalt are killed. Romeo is banished from
Verona.

1 *retire*: go indoors.
2 *Capels*: Capulets.
  *abroad*: out of doors.
3 *scape*: avoid.
  *brawl*: quarrel.
4 *these hot days*: The play's action takes
  place in the middle of July (see
  *1, 3, 16–17*).
5–29 *Thou . . . quarrelling*: Mercutio
  tells us more about himself than
  about Benvolio.
6 *claps me*: throws.
7–8 *by . . . cup*: under the influence of
  the second drink.
8 *draws him*: draws his sword.
9 *drawer*: tapster, barman.

11 *Jack*: fellow.
  *mood*: anger, quarrelsome mood.
12 *moved to be moody*: provoked to be
  angry.
13 *moody to be moved*: angry at being
  provoked.

15 *and*: if.
  *two*: Mercutio plays on Benvolio's 'to'
  (line 14).

20 *hazel eyes*: eyes the colour of a hazel
  nut.

22 *meat*: food.
23 *addle*: rotten.

## SCENE 1

*A public place: enter* Mercutio *and his* Page,
Benvolio *and* Men

**Benvolio**
I pray thee, good Mercutio, let's retire:
The day is hot, the Capels are abroad,
And if we meet we shall not scape a brawl,
For now, these hot days, is the mad blood stirring.
   **Mercutio**
5 Thou art like one of these fellows that, when he enters
the confines of a tavern, claps me his sword upon the
table, and says 'God send me no need of thee!'; and by
the operation of the second cup draws him on the
drawer, when indeed there is no need.
   **Benvolio**
10 Am I like such a fellow?
   **Mercutio**
Come, come, thou art as hot a Jack in thy mood as any
in Italy, and as soon moved to be moody, and as soon
moody to be moved.
   **Benvolio**
And what to?
   **Mercutio**
15 Nay, and there were two such, we should have none
shortly, for one would kill the other. Thou? why, thou
wilt quarrel with a man that hath a hair more or a hair
less in his beard than thou hast; thou wilt quarrel with a
man for cracking nuts, having no other reason but
20 because thou hast hazel eyes. What eye but such an eye
would spy out such a quarrel? Thy head is as full of
quarrels as an egg is full of meat, and yet thy head hath
been beaten as addle as an egg for quarrelling. Thou
hast quarrelled with a man for coughing in the street,
25 because he hath wakened thy dog that hath lain asleep

26 *fall out*: quarrel.

27 *his new doublet*: the sleeveless jacket he has designed (perhaps for the Easter fashions!).

28 *tying . . . riband*: using old ribbon (as shoelaces) for the new shoes he has supplied.

29 *tutor me from*: lecture me about.

30 *apt*: ready, prone.

30-1 *any . . . quarter*: I could sell my life outright to any man who would buy it for as little as an hour and a quarter (because I would expect to be dead by then).

31 *fee-simple*: a legal term for 'absolute possession'.

32s.d. *Petruchio*: This non-speaking character is probably the 'young Petruchio' seen by the Nurse at the Capulet's ball (*1*, 5, 130).

40 *occasion*: excuse, provocation (see *2*, 4, 24–5note).

42 *consortest*: keep company.

43 *Consort*: a company of hired musicians; Mercutio deliberately mistakes Tybalt's meaning.

45 *fiddlestick*: bow (in this case, his sword).

46 *'Zounds*: by god's wounds.

47 *haunt*: meeting place.

49 *coldly*: calmly.

in the sun. Didst thou not fall out with a tailor for wearing his new doublet before Easter? with another for tying his new shoes with old riband? and yet thou wilt tutor me from quarrelling.

**Benvolio**

30 And I were so apt to quarrel as thou art, any man should buy the fee-simple of my life for an hour and a quarter.

**Mercutio**

The fee-simple? O simple!

*Enter* Tybalt, Petruchio, *and others*

**Benvolio**

By my head, here comes the Capulets.

**Mercutio**

By my heel, I care not.

**Tybalt**

35 Follow me close, for I will speak to them.

Gentlemen, good den, a word with one of you.

**Mercutio**

And but one word with one of us? couple it with something, make it a word and a blow.

**Tybalt**

You shall find me apt enough to that, sir, and you will

40 give me occasion.

**Mercutio**

Could you not take some occasion without giving?

**Tybalt**

Mercutio, thou consortest with Romeo.

**Mercutio**

Consort? what, dost thou make us minstrels? And thou make minstrels of us, look to hear nothing but discords.

45 Here's my fiddlestick, here's that shall make you dance.

'Zounds, consort!

**Benvolio**

We talk here in the public haunt of men:

Either withdraw unto some private place,

Or reason coldly of your grievances,

50 Or else depart; here all eyes gaze on us.

**Mercutio**
Men's eyes were made to look, and let them gaze;
I will not budge for no man's pleasure, I.

*Enter* Romeo

**Tybalt**
Well, peace be with you, sir, here comes my man.
   **Mercutio**
But I'll be hang'd, sir, if he wear your livery.
55 Marry, go before to field, he'll be your follower;
Your worship in that sense may call him man.
   **Tybalt**
Romeo, the love I bear thee can afford
No better term than this: thou art a villain.
   **Romeo**
Tybalt, the reason that I have to love thee
60 Doth much excuse the appertaining rage
To such a greeting. Villain am I none;
Therefore farewell, I see thou knowest me not.
   **Tybalt**
Boy, this shall not excuse the injuries
That thou hast done me, therefore turn and draw.
   **Romeo**
65 I do protest I never injuried thee,
But love thee better than thou canst devise,
Till thou shalt know the reason of my love;
And so, good Capulet, which name I tender
As dearly as mine own, be satisfied.
   **Mercutio**
70 O calm, dishonourable, vile submission!
'Alla stoccata' carries it away. [*Draws*]
Tybalt, you rat-catcher, will you walk?
   **Tybalt**
What wouldst thou have with me?
   **Mercutio**
Good King of Cats, nothing but one of your nine lives
75 that I mean to make bold withal, and as you shall use
me hereafter, dry-beat the rest of the eight. Will you
pluck your sword out of his pilcher by the ears? Make
haste, lest mine be about your ears ere it be out.

53 *my man*: the man I am looking for— but Mercutio deliberately misunderstands.
54 *livery*: servant's badge or uniform.
55 *go . . . field*: if you will lead the way to the duelling-ground.

58 *villain*: scoundrel, peasant (a very serious insult that would call for instant reprisal).

60–1 *the . . . greeting*: the anger appropriate for such a form of address.

63 *Boy*: A term of contempt.

65 *injuried*: injured (a variant form).
66 *devise*: imagine.

68 *tender*: value.

71 *Alla stoccata*: at the thrust (an Italian fencing term). Mercutio uses it as a name for Tybalt.
   *carries it away*: has won.
72 *walk*: i.e. walk away, to fight a duel.
74 *King of Cats*: see note to *2*, 4, 19.
   *nine lives*: in England, cats are proverbially said to have nine lives.
75 *make bold withal*: do as I please with.
75–6 *use me*: deal with me.
76 *dry-beat*: beat without drawing blood.
77 *pilcher*: case.
   *by the ears*: without ceremony.
78 *about your ears*: attacking you.

**Tybalt**
I am for you. [*Drawing*]
     **Romeo**
80 Gentle Mercutio, put thy rapier up.
     **Mercutio**
Come, sir, your 'passado'.

*They fight*

**Romeo**
Draw, Benvolio, beat down their weapons.
Gentlemen, for shame forbear this outrage!
Tybalt, Mercutio, the prince expressly hath
85 Forbid this bandying in Verona streets.

Romeo *steps between them*

Hold, Tybalt! Good Mercutio!

Tybalt *under* Romeo's *arm thrusts* Mercutio *in*

[*Away* Tybalt *with his followers*

81 *your passado*: the fencing thrust
you're so proud of (see
*2*, 4, 25–6note).

83 *forebear*: give over, stop.

85 *bandying*: skirmishing, fighting.

86s.d.   *thrusts . . . in*: thrusts his rapier
into Mercutio.

**Mercutio**

I am hurt.

A plague a'both houses! I am sped.

Is he gone and hath nothing?

**Benvolio**

What, art thou hurt?

**Mercutio**

Ay, ay, a scratch, a scratch, marry, 'tis enough.

90 Where is my page? Go, villain, fetch a surgeon.

[*Exit* Page

**Romeo**

Courage, man, the hurt cannot be much.

**Mercutio**

No, 'tis not so deep as a well, nor so wide as a church-
door, but 'tis enough, 'twill serve. Ask for me tomorrow,
and you shall find me a grave man. I am peppered, I

95 warrant, for this world. A plague a'both your houses!
'Zounds, a dog, a rat, a mouse, a cat, to scratch a man to
death! a braggart, a rogue, a villain, that fights by the
book of arithmetic. Why the dev'l came you between us!
I was hurt under your arm.

**Romeo**

100 I thought all for the best.

**Mercutio**

Help me into some house, Benvolio,

Or I shall faint. A plague a'both your houses!

They have made worms' meat of me. I have it,

And soundly too. Your houses!   [*Exit with* Benvolio

**Romeo**

105 This gentleman, the prince's near ally,

My very friend, hath got his mortal hurt

In my behalf; my reputation stain'd

With Tybalt's slander—Tybalt, that an hour

Hath been my cousin. O sweet Juliet,

110 Thy beauty hath made me effeminate,

And in my temper soften'd valour's steel!

*Enter* Benvolio

---

87  *a'both*: on both.
   *sped*: done for, killed.
88  *nothing*: no wound.

93  *serve*: i.e. to kill me.
94  *peppered*: finished.

98  *book of arithmetic*: textbook of
   fencing by numbers.
99  *under your arm*: Mercutio believes
   that Romeo's intervention gave Tybalt
   the chance to kill him.

103  *worms' meat*: a dead body.
103–4  *I have . . . too*: I have been fatally
   wounded, and no mistake.

105  *ally*: kinsman.

106  *very*: true.
   *mortal hurt*: deadly wound.

108  *slander*: insults.

111  *in . . . steel*: weakened the steely
   courage of my disposition; Romeo
   makes a wry play on the technique of
   'tempering' steel.

113 *aspir'd*: mounted up to.
114 *untimely*: prematurely.

115 *This . . . depend*: the fatal
consequences of today's events hang
upon what happens in the future
('moe days').
116 *others*: other days.

119 *Away . . . lenity*: the mercy that shows
consideration (for kinship with Tybalt)
can go back to heaven (where it
belongs).
120 *conduct*: guide.
122 *late*: recently.

124 *staying*: waiting.

126 *consort*: accompany.

129 *up*: aroused.
130 *amaz'd*: bewildered.
*doom thee*: condemn you to.

132 *fool*: plaything.

**Benvolio**
O Romeo, Romeo, brave Mercutio is dead.
That gallant spirit hath aspir'd the clouds,
Which too untimely here did scorn the earth.
**Romeo**
115 This day's black fate on moe days doth depend,
This but begins the woe others must end.

*Enter* Tybalt

**Benvolio**
Here comes the furious Tybalt back again.
**Romeo**
Again, in triumph, and Mercutio slain?
Away to heaven, respective lenity,
120 And fire-ey'd fury be my conduct now!
Now, Tybalt, take the 'villain' back again
That late thou gavest me, for Mercutio's soul
Is but a little way above our heads,
Staying for thine to keep him company:
125 Either thou or I, or both, must go with him.
**Tybalt**
Thou wretched boy, that didst consort him here,
Shalt with him hence.
**Romeo**
　　　　　　　　　This shall determine that.

*They fight; Tybalt falls*

**Benvolio**
Romeo, away, be gone!
The citizens are up, and Tybalt slain.
130 Stand not amaz'd, the prince will doom thee death
If thou art taken. Hence be gone, away!
**Romeo**
O, I am fortune's fool.
**Benvolio**
　　　　　　　　　Why dost thou stay?
　　　　　　　　　　　　　[*Exit* Romeo

*Enter* Citizens *and* Officers *of the Watch*

**Officer**
Which way ran he that kill'd Mercutio?
Tybalt, that murderer, which way ran he?
**Benvolio**
135 There lies that Tybalt.
**Officer**
                                    Up, sir, go with me;
I charge thee in the prince's name obey.

*Enter* Prince, *old* Montague, Capulet, *their* Wives,
*and all*

**Prince**
Where are the vile beginners of this fray?
**Benvolio**
O noble prince, I can discover all
The unlucky manage of this fatal brawl;
140 There lies the man, slain by young Romeo,
That slew thy kinsman, brave Mercutio.
**Lady Capulet**
Tybalt, my cousin! O my brother's child!
O Prince! O husband! O, the blood is spill'd
Of my dear kinsman. Prince, as thou art true,
145 For blood of ours, shed blood of Montague.
O cousin, cousin!
**Prince**
Benvolio, who began this bloody fray?
**Benvolio**
Tybalt, here slain, whom Romeo's hand did slay.
Romeo, that spoke him fair, bid him bethink
150 How nice the quarrel was, and urg'd withal
Your high displeasure; all this, uttered
With gentle breath, calm look, knees humbly bow'd,
Could not take truce with the unruly spleen
Of Tybalt deaf to peace, but that he tilts
155 With piercing steel at bold Mercutio's breast,
Who, all as hot, turns deadly point to point,
And with a martial scorn, with one hand beats
Cold death aside, and with the other sends

138 *discover*: reveal.
139 *manage*: conduct.

149 *spoke him fair*: spoke politely to him.
*bethink*: consider.
150 *nice*: trivial.
*urg'd withal*: argued in addition.
151 *uttered*: utterèd.
153 *take truce*: make peace.
*spleen*: temper.
154 *but that*: on the contrary.
*tilts*: thrusts.
156 *all as hot*: just as angry.
157–8 *with one . . . other*: parries the
death-dealing strokes with one hand,
and returns them with the other;
Mercutio was fighting with dagger and
sword.

160 *Retorts it*: sends it (death) back again to him.

164 *envious*: malicious.
*hit the life*: killed.
165 *stout*: brave.

167 *entertain'd*: thought about.

173 *Affection . . . true*: Lady Capulet's accusation, although exaggerated, is not entirely unjust: Benvolio, stressing Mercutio's kinship with the Prince, ignored his provocation and implied that Tybalt was the sole aggressor, 'deaf to peace'.

179 *Who . . . owe*: who then should pay the cost of Mercutio's life.
*dear*: (a) beloved; (b) precious.

181 *concludes but*: only finishes.

182 *for that offence*: i.e. for taking the law into his own hands.

184 *I . . . proceeding*: I am personally concerned in your emotional reactions.
185 *My blood*: Mercutio was related to the Prince.
186 *amerce*: punish.
187 *loss of mine*: my loss.
189 *purchase out*: buy pardon for.

193 *Mercy . . . kill*: in pardoning murderers, mercy only leads to more murders.

It back to Tybalt, whose dexterity
160 Retorts it. Romeo he cries aloud,
'Hold, friends! friends, part!' and swifter than his tongue,
His agile arm beats down their fatal points,
And 'twixt them rushes; underneath whose arm
An envious thrust from Tybalt hit the life
165 Of stout Mercutio, and then Tybalt fled;
But by and by comes back to Romeo,
Who had but newly entertain'd revenge,
And to't they go like lightning, for, ere I
Could draw to part them, was stout Tybalt slain;
170 And as he fell, did Romeo turn and fly.
This is the truth, or let Benvolio die.
     **Lady Capulet**
He is a kinsman to the Montague,
Affection makes him false, he speaks not true:
Some twenty of them fought in this black strife,
175 And all those twenty could but kill one life.
I beg for justice, which thou, Prince, must give:
Romeo slew Tybalt, Romeo must not live.
     **Prince**
Romeo slew him, he slew Mercutio;
Who now the price of his dear blood doth owe?
     **Montague**
180 Not Romeo, Prince, he was Mercutio's friend;
His fault concludes but what the law should end,
The life of Tybalt.
     **Prince**
             And for that offence
Immediately we do exile him hence.
I have an interest in your hearts' proceeding:
185 My blood for your rude brawls doth lie a-bleeding;
But I'll amerce you with so strong a fine
That you shall all repent the loss of mine.
I will be deaf to pleading and excuses,
Nor tears nor prayers shall purchase out abuses:
190 Therefore use none. Let Romeo hence in haste,
Else, when he is found, that hour is his last.
Bear hence this body, and attend our will:
Mercy but murders, pardoning those that kill.

                               [*Exeunt*

**Act 3 Scene 2**
Juliet is eagerly waiting for her husband, but the Nurse brings bad news.

1 *apace*: fast.
*fiery-footed steeds*: horses drawing the chariot of Phoebus Apollo, the sun-god.
2 *lodging*: resting-place.
3 *Phaëton*: the son of Phoebus Apollo, who borrowed his father's chariot but could not control the horses.
5 *close curtain*: curtain (of a four-poster bed) ensuring privacy.
*love-performing*: suitable for performing acts of love.
6 *runaways' eyes*: the eyes of (a) the horses of the sun, (b) any night-wanderers.
*wink*: close in sleep; pretend not to see.
9 *if . . . blind*: See *1, 1, 165*note.
10 *best agrees*: is most appropriate for.
*civil*: sober, respectable.
12 *learn*: teach.
*lose . . . match*: Juliet will lose her virginity, but win a husband.
14–15 *Hood . . . mantle*: cover my blushes with your darkness; Juliet uses the language of falconry (compare *2, 2, 158–9*).
*Hood*: blindfold (like an untrained hawk).
*unmanned*: untamed (not trained by a man); husbandless.
*bating*: fluttering.
15 *mantle*: cloak.
15–16 *strange . . . modesty*: shy love becomes courageous, and thinks the sexual act of true lovers is pure chastity.
26 *mansion*: splendid dwelling place.
27 *possess'd*: taken possession of.
*I am sold*: Juliet sees herself as another 'mansion'.

# Scene 2

*Capulet's house: enter* Juliet *alone*

**Juliet**
Gallop apace, you fiery-footed steeds,
Towards Phoebus' lodging; such a waggoner
As Phaëton would whip you to the west,
And bring in cloudy night immediately.
5 Spread thy close curtain, love-performing Night,
That runaways' eyes may wink, and Romeo
Leap to these arms, untalk'd of and unseen:
Lovers can see to do their amorous rites
By their own beauties, or if love be blind,
10 It best agrees with night. Come, civil Night,
Thou sober-suited matron all in black,
And learn me how to lose a winning match,
Play'd for a pair of stainless maidenhoods.
Hood my unmann'd blood, bating in my cheeks,
15 With thy black mantle, till strange love grow bold,
Think true love acted simple modesty.
Come, Night, come, Romeo, come, thou day in night,
For thou wilt lie upon the wings of night,
Whiter than new snow upon a raven's back.
20 Come, gentle Night, come, loving, black-brow'd Night,
Give me my Romeo, and when I shall die,
Take him and cut him out in little stars,
And he will make the face of heaven so fine
That all the world will be in love with night,
25 And pay no worship to the garish sun.
O, I have bought the mansion of a love,
But not possess'd it, and though I am sold,
Not yet enjoy'd. So tedious is this day
As is the night before some festival
30 To an impatient child that hath new robes
And may not wear them. O, here comes my Nurse,

31s.d.  *in her lap*: under her cloak.

*Enter* Nurse, *with the ladder of cords in her lap*

And she brings news, and every tongue that speaks
But Romeo's name speaks heavenly eloquence.
Now, Nurse, what news? What hast thou there? the
cords

34  *cords*: rope-ladder.

35  That Romeo bid thee fetch?
    **Nurse**

Ay, ay, the cords.

*Throws them down*

**Juliet**
Ay me, what news? Why dost thou wring thy hands?
    **Nurse**

37  *weraday*: alas.
38  *undone*: ruined.

Ah weraday, he's dead, he's dead, he's dead!
We are undone, lady, we are undone.
Alack the day, he's gone, he's kill'd, he's dead!
    **Juliet**

40  *envious*: spiteful.

40  Can heaven be so envious?
    **Nurse**

Romeo can,
Though heaven cannot. O Romeo, Romeo!
Who ever would have thought it? Romeo!
    **Juliet**
What devil are thou that dost torment me thus?
This torture should be roar'd in dismal hell.

44  *torture*: i.e. the Nurse's manner of
    telling her news.
45–50  *'ay' . . . say 'ay'*: Juliet plays
    hysterically on 'ay' (= yes), 'I' (the
    letter), 'I' (the pronoun), and 'eye'.
47  *cockatrice*: a fabulous serpent whose
    glance could kill.
49  *those eyes*: i.e. Romeo's eyes, closed
    in death.

45  Hath Romeo slain himself? Say thou but 'ay',
And that bare vowel 'I' shall poison more
Than the death-darting eye of cockatrice.
I am not I, if there be such an 'ay',
Or those eyes shut, that makes thee answer 'ay'.

51  *determine*: decide.
    *weal*: happiness.

50  If he be slain, say 'ay', or if not, 'no':
Brief sounds determine my weal or woe.
    **Nurse**
I saw the wound, I saw it with mine eyes

53  *God . . . mark*: forgive me for saying
    this; an apologetic exclamation.
54  *corse*: corpse.

(God save the mark!), here on his manly breast:
A piteous corse, a bloody piteous corse,

55  Pale, pale as ashes, all bedaub'd in blood,

56  *gore*: partially congealed blood.
    *sounded*: swooned.

All in gore blood; I sounded at the sight.

57 *bankrout*: bankrupt; Juliet feels that
her heart has lost everything that is
precious.
59 *Vile earth*: i.e. her body.
*resign*: surrender.
*motion*: physical movement.
60 *heavy*: sorrowful.

62 *honest*: honourable.

64 *so contrary*: i.e. from Romeo's death
to Tybalt's.

67 *dreadful . . . doom*: let the last
trumpet announce the Day of
Judgement ('at the last trump . . . the
trumpet shall sound', 1 Corinthians
15:52).
69–70 *banished*: banishèd.

73–85 *O serpent . . . palace*: Juliet is
bewildered by the apparent contrast
between appearances and reality.
74 *keep*: hide in.

77 *Despised*: despisèd.
*show*: appearance.
78 *Just opposite*: the exact opposite.
*justly seem'st*: truly appeared.
79 *damned*: damnèd.
81 *bower*: enclose.

87 *naught*: nothing.
88 *aqua-vitae*: 'water of life'; a modern
equivalent is brandy.

**Juliet**
O break, my heart, poor bankrout, break at once!
To prison, eyes, ne'er look on liberty!
Vile earth, to earth resign, end motion here,
60 And thou and Romeo press one heavy bier!
**Nurse**
O Tybalt, Tybalt, the best friend I had!
O courteous Tybalt, honest gentleman,
That ever I should live to see thee dead!
**Juliet**
What storm is this that blows so contrary?
65 Is Romeo slaughter'd? and is Tybalt dead?
My dearest cousin, and my dearer lord?
Then, dreadful trumpet, sound the general doom,
For who is living, if those two are gone?
**Nurse**
Tybalt is gone and Romeo banished,
70 Romeo that kill'd him, he is banished.
**Juliet**
O God, did Romeo's hand shed Tybalt's blood?
**Nurse**
It did, it did, alas the day, it did!
**Juliet**
O serpent heart, hid with a flow'ring face!
Did ever dragon keep so fair a cave?
75 Beautiful tyrant, fiend angelical!
Dove-feather'd raven, wolvish-ravening lamb!
Despised substance of divinest show!
Just opposite to what thou justly seem'st,
A damned saint, an honourable villain!
80 O nature, what hadst thou to do in hell
When thou didst bower the spirit of a fiend
In mortal paradise of such sweet flesh?
Was ever book containing such vile matter
So fairly bound? O that deceit should dwell
85 In such a gorgeous palace!
**Nurse**
                                There's no trust,
No faith, no honesty in men, all perjur'd,
All forsworn, all naught, all dissemblers.
Ah, where's my man? Give me some aqua-vitae;

These griefs, these woes, these sorrows make me old.
90 Shame come to Romeo!
　　**Juliet**
　　　　　　　　　Blister'd be thy tongue
For such a wish! he was not born to shame:
Upon his brow shame is asham'd to sit;
For 'tis a throne where honour may be crown'd
Sole monarch of the universal earth.
95 O what a beast was I to chide at him!
　　**Nurse**
Will you speak well of him that kill'd your cousin?
　　**Juliet**
Shall I speak ill of him that is my husband?

98 *poor my lord*: my poor lord.
*smooth*: speak well of.

Ah, poor my lord, what tongue shall smooth thy name,
When I, thy three-hours wife, have mangl'd it?
100 But wherefore, villain, didst thou kill my cousin?
That villain cousin would have kill'd my husband.

102 *native spring*: source—i.e. her eyes.
103 *tributary drops*: tears paid as tribute.
104 *mistaking*: i.e. her eyes have mistaken a joyful occasion (Romeo's survival) for a sad one.
105 *that . . . slain*: whom Tybalt wanted to slay.

Back, foolish tears, back to your native spring,
Your tributary drops belong to woe,
Which you mistaking offer up to joy.
105 My husband lives that Tybalt would have slain,
And Tybalt's dead that would have slain my husband:
All this is comfort, wherefore weep I then?
Some word there was, worser than Tybalt's death,
That murder'd me; I would forget it fain,

109 *forget it fain*: gladly forget it.
110 *presses*: pushes its way.
111 *damned*: damnèd.
112–13 *banished*: banishèd.

110 But O, it presses to my memory,
Like damned guilty deeds to sinners' minds:
'Tybalt is dead, and Romeo banished.'
That 'banished', that one word 'banished',
Hath slain ten thousand Tybalts. Tybalt's death
115 Was woe enough if it had ended there;
Or if sour woe delights in fellowship,
And needly will be rank'd with other griefs,

116 *if . . . fellowship*: if one sorrow likes to have another for company.
117 *needly*: of necessity.
*rank'd*: joined.

Why follow'd not, when she said 'Tybalt's dead',
'Thy father' or 'thy mother', nay, or both,

120 *modern*: ordinary.
*mov'd*: caused.
121 *with . . . following*: following, like a rearguard, the news of Tybalt's death.
122–4 *banished*: banishèd.

120 Which modern lamentation might have mov'd?
But with a rear-ward following Tybalt's death,
'Romeo is banished': to speak that word,
Is father, mother, Tybalt, Romeo, Juliet,
All slain, all dead. 'Romeo is banished!'

126 *that word's death*: the death which
that word brings.
*sound*: express, measure.

130 *spent*: shed.

132 *beguil'd*: cheated.

135 *maid*: virgin.
*maiden-widowed*: widowèd; a virgin
and a widow.

139 *wot*: know.

125 There is no end, no limit, measure, bound,
In that word's death, no words can that woe sound.
Where is my father and my mother, Nurse?
    **Nurse**
Weeping and wailing over Tybalt's corse.
Will you go to them? I will bring you thither.
    **Juliet**
130 Wash they his wounds with tears? mine shall be spent,
When theirs are dry, for Romeo's banishment.
Take up those cords. Poor ropes, you are beguil'd,
Both you and I, for Romeo is exil'd.
He made you for a highway to my bed,
135 But I, a maid, die maiden-widowed.
Come, cords, come, Nurse, I'll to my wedding bed,
And death, not Romeo, take my maidenhead!
    **Nurse**
Hie to your chamber. I'll find Romeo
To comfort you, I wot well where he is.
140 Hark ye, your Romeo will be here at night.
I'll to him, he is hid at Lawrence' cell.
    **Juliet**
O find him! Give this ring to my true knight,
And bid him come to take his last farewell.     [*Exeunt*

**Act 3 Scene 3**
Friar Lawrence tries to console Romeo and
find a solution for the terrible problems that
have arisen.

1 *fearful*: frightened.
2 *enamour'd of*: in love with.
*parts*: nature, characters.

4 *doom*: judgement.
5 *craves*: desires.
*acquaintance at my hand*: to be
introduced to me.

# SCENE 3

*Friar Lawrence's cell: enter* Friar Lawrence

**Friar Lawrence**
Romeo, come forth, come forth, thou fearful man:
Affliction is enamour'd of thy parts,
And thou art wedded to calamity.

*Enter* Romeo

**Romeo**
Father, what news? What is the prince's doom?
5 What sorrow craves acquaintance at my hand,
That I yet know not?

**Friar Lawrence**

Too familiar
Is my dear son with such sour company!
I bring thee tidings of the prince's doom.

**Romeo**

What less than doomsday is the prince's doom?

**Friar Lawrence**

10 A gentler judgement vanish'd from his lips:
Not body's death, but body's banishment.

**Romeo**

Ha, banishment? be merciful, say 'death':
For exile hath more terror in his look,
Much more than death. Do not say 'banishment'!

**Friar Lawrence**

15 Here from Verona art thou banished.
Be patient, for the world is broad and wide.

**Romeo**

There is no world without Verona walls,
But purgatory, torture, hell itself:
Hence 'banished' is banish'd from the world,
20 And world's exile is death; then 'banished'
Is death misterm'd. Calling death 'banished',
Thou cut'st my head off with a golden axe,
And smilest upon the stroke that murders me.

**Friar Lawrence**

O deadly sin! O rude unthankfulness!
25 Thy fault our law calls death, but the kind prince,
Taking thy part, hath rush'd aside the law,
And turn'd that black word 'death' to 'banishment'.
This is dear mercy, and thou seest it not.

**Romeo**

'Tis torture, and not mercy. Heaven is here
30 Where Juliet lives, and every cat and dog
And little mouse, every unworthy thing,
Live here in heaven, and may look on her,
But Romeo may not. More validity,
More honourable state, more courtship lives
35 In carrion flies than Romeo; they may seize
On the white wonder of dear Juliet's hand,
And steal immortal blessing from her lips,

8   *tidings*: news.

9   *doomsday*: the Day of Judgement (i.e. death).

10   *vanish'd*: issued.

13   *hath . . . look*: seems more terrifying.

15–21   *banished*: banishèd.

17   *without*: outside.

19   *Hence 'banished'*: banishèd; to be banished from here (Verona).
20   *world's exile*: exile from the world.
21   *death misterm'd*: the wrong name for what is in fact death.
21–2   *Calling . . . axe*: to speak of death as 'banishment' is like cutting off a man's head with a golden axe: it is still fatal.

25   *fault*: crime.
     *calls*: punishes with.
26   *rush'd*: swept.

33   *validity*: value.
34   *courtship*: courtly behaviour.
35   *carrion flies*: flies that feed on dead flesh.

38 *vestal*: virgin.

39 *Still blush*: are always blushing.
   *as . . . sin*: as if they think it is a sin
   to touch each other.
40–70 *banished*: banishèd.

44 *sharp-ground*: sharpened by grinding.

45 *sudden mean of death*: quick way to
   kill myself.
   *ne'er so mean*: however base.

47 *damned*: damnèd.

48 *Howling attends it*: the anguished
   screams of damned souls accompany
   that word.

49 *a divine*: a priest.
   *ghostly*: spiritual.

50 *sin-absolver*: one who has the power to
   absolve sins.
   *my friend profess'd*: one who claims to
   be my friend.

51 *mangle*: wound, tear in pieces.

52 *fond*: foolish.

55 *Adversity's sweet milk*: the soothing
   comfort for hardship.

57 *Yet 'banished'*: do you still use the
   word 'banished'.
   *Hang up*: throw away (unused suits of
   armour were hung on the walls of
   palaces).

59 *Displant*: transplant.

60 *prevails not*: is of no use.

61 *no ears*: i.e. to listen to good counsel.

62 *no eyes*: i.e. to see someone's
   distress.

63 *dispute . . . estate*: discuss your
   present situation.

66 *An hour but married*: married for no
   more than an hour.
   *murdered*: murderèd.

Who even in pure and vestal modesty
Still blush, as thinking their own kisses sin;
40 But Romeo may not, he is banished.
Flies may do this, but I from this must fly;
They are free men, but I am banished:
And sayest thou yet that exile is not death?
Hadst thou no poison mix'd, no sharp-ground knife,
45 No sudden mean of death, though ne'er so mean,
But 'banished' to kill me? 'Banished'?
O Friar, the damned use that word in hell;
Howling attends it. How hast thou the heart,
Being a divine, a ghostly confessor,
50 A sin-absolver, and my friend profess'd,
To mangle me with that word 'banished'?
   **Friar Lawrence**
Thou fond mad man, hear me a little speak.
   **Romeo**
O thou wilt speak again of banishment.
   **Friar Lawrence**
I'll give thee armour to keep off that word:
55 Adversity's sweet milk, philosophy,
To comfort thee though thou art banished.
   **Romeo**
Yet 'banished'? Hang up philosophy!
Unless philosophy can make a Juliet,
Displant a town, reverse a prince's doom,
60 It helps not, it prevails not; talk no more.
   **Friar Lawrence**
O then I see that mad men have no ears.
   **Romeo**
How should they when that wise men have no eyes?
   **Friar Lawrence**
Let me dispute with thee of thy estate.
   **Romeo**
Thou canst not speak of that thou dost not feel.
65 Wert thou as young as I, Juliet thy love,
An hour but married, Tybalt murdered,
Doting like me, and like me banished,
Then mightst thou speak, then mightst thou tear thy
   hair,

70 *Taking the measure*: measuring the
   length.

70s.d. *within*: offstage.

71 *one*: someone.

72 *infold*: wrap itself round.

75 *taken*: captured.
   *Stay a while*: wait a moment (the Friar
   speaks to the person knocking).

77 *simpleness*: folly.

And fall upon the ground as I do now,
70    Taking the measure of an unmade grave.

*Enter* Nurse *within and knock*

**Friar Lawrence**
Arise, one knocks. Good Romeo, hide thyself.
**Romeo**
Not I, unless the breath of heart-sick groans
Mist-like infold me from the search of eyes.

*Knock*

**Friar Lawrence**
Hark how they knock!—Who's there?—Romeo, arise,
75    Thou wilt be taken.—Stay a while!—Stand up;

*Loud knock*

Run to my study.—By and by!—God's will,
What simpleness is this?—I come, I come!

*Knock*

Who knocks so hard? whence come you? what's your
   will?
**Nurse**
[*Within*] Let me come in, and you shall know my
   errand:
80    I come from Lady Juliet.
**Friar Lawrence**
                    Welcome then.

*Unlocks the door*

*Enter* Nurse

**Nurse**
O holy Friar, O tell me, holy Friar,
Where's my lady's lord? where's Romeo?

**Friar Lawrence**
There on the ground, with his own tears made drunk.
   **Nurse**
O he is even in my mistress' case,
85 Just in her case. O woeful sympathy!
Piteous predicament! even so lies she,
Blubb'ring and weeping, weeping and blubb'ring.
Stand up, stand up, stand, and you be a man;
For Juliet's sake, for her sake, rise and stand;
90 Why should you fall into so deep an O?
   **Romeo**
Nurse!

*He rises*

   **Nurse**
Ah, sir, ah, sir, death's the end of all.
   **Romeo**
Spakest thou of Juliet? how is it with her?
Doth not she think me an old murderer,
95 Now I have stain'd the childhood of our joy
With blood remov'd but little from her own?
Where is she? and how doth she? and what says
My conceal'd lady to our cancell'd love?
   **Nurse**
O she says nothing, sir, but weeps and weeps,
100 And now falls on her bed, and then starts up,
And Tybalt calls, and then on Romeo cries,
And then down falls again.
   **Romeo**
                              As if that name,
Shot from the deadly level of a gun,
Did murder her, as that name's cursed hand
105 Murder'd her kinsman. O tell me, Friar, tell me,
In what vile part of this anatomy
Doth my name lodge? Tell me, that I may sack
The hateful mansion.

*He offers to stab himself, and* Nurse *snatches the
dagger away*

84 *even . . . case*: in just the same state
   as my mistress.
85 *woeful sympathy*: shared misery.

88 *and*: if.

90 *so deep an O*: so profound a lament.

93 *Spakest*: did you speak.
   *how is it with her*: how is she.
94 *old*: experienced.

96 *remov'd but little*: not very far from.

98 *My conceal'd lady*: my secret wife.
   *cancell'd*: rendered void, nullified (a
   legal term).

100 *starts*: jumps.
101 *cries*: exclaims.

103 *level*: aim.
104 *cursed*: cursèd.

106 *anatomy*: body.
107 *lodge*: reside.
   *sack*: ransack.
108 *mansion*: dwelling place.

108s.d. *offers*: tries.

## Friar Lawrence

                                    Hold thy desperate hand!
Art thou a man? thy form cries out thou art;
110 Thy tears are womanish, thy wild acts denote
The unreasonable fury of a beast.
Unseemly woman in a seeming man,
And ill-beseeming beast in seeming both,
Thou hast amaz'd me. By my holy order,
115 I thought thy disposition better temper'd.
Hast thou slain Tybalt? wilt thou slay thyself,
And slay thy lady that in thy life lives,
By doing damned hate upon thyself?
Why rail'st thou on thy birth? the heaven and earth?
120 Since birth, and heaven, and earth, all three do meet
In thee at once, which thou at once wouldst lose.
Fie, fie, thou sham'st thy shape, thy love, thy wit,
Which like a usurer abound'st in all,
And usest none in that true use indeed
125 Which should bedeck thy shape, thy love, thy wit:
Thy noble shape is but a form of wax,
Digressing from the valour of a man;
Thy dear love sworn but hollow perjury,
Killing that love which thou hast vow'd to cherish;
130 Thy wit, that ornament to shape and love,
Misshapen in the conduct of them both,
Like powder in a skilless soldier's flask,
Is set afire by thine own ignorance,
And thou dismember'd with thine own defence.
135 What, rouse thee, man! thy Juliet is alive,
For whose dear sake thou wast but lately dead:
There art thou happy. Tybalt would kill thee,
But thou slewest Tybalt: there art thou happy.
The law that threaten'd death becomes thy friend,
140 And turns it to exile: there art thou happy.
A pack of blessings light upon thy back,
Happiness courts thee in her best array,
But like a mishaved and sullen wench,
Thou pouts upon thy fortune and thy love:
145 Take heed, take heed, for such die miserable.
Go get thee to thy love as was decreed,
Ascend her chamber, hence and comfort her;

109 *cries out*: declares.

111 *unreasonable*: unreasoning; the ability to reason distinguishes man from the beasts.
112–13 *Unseemly . . . both*: shameful behaviour for a woman, in someone who looks like a man, makes a monstrous beast, apparently both male and female.
114 *my holy order*: the Order of St Francis.
115 *temper'd*: balanced, disciplined.
117 *in . . . lives*: lives only because you live.
118 *doing . . . thyself*: committing a deadly sin by killing yourself. *damned*: damnèd.
119 *Why rail'st thou*: why do you curse. *birth . . . earth*: parentage, soul (the heavenly part), and body.
122 *sham'st*: abuse. *shape . . . wit*: form as a man (made in the image of God), sworn faith to Juliet, and power of reason.
123–4 *Which . . . indeed*: you're like a usurer—rich in all of these, and using none of them properly.
125 *bedeck*: improve, ornament.
126 *form of wax*: wax image (not a real man).
127 *Digressing . . . man*: i.e. if it deviates from manly fortitude.
128 *Thy . . . sworn*: the sincere love that you promised Juliet. *hollow*: empty.
129 *Killing*: if you kill.
131 *Misshapen*: wrongly directed. *conduct*: guidance.
132 *powder . . . flask*: gunpowder carried by an incompetent soldier in a powder-container.
134 *dismember'd . . . defence*: blown to pieces by the very thing that should protect you.
136 *wast . . . dead*: i.e. just now tried to kill yourself.
137 *happy*: fortunate.
141 *light*: alights.
143 *mishaved*: mishavèd; naughty.

146 *decreed*: determined.

148 *the Watch be set*: The city gates would
   be locked when the night guards took
   up their positions.

151 *blaze*: proclaim, announce.
   *friends*: relatives (of both families).

157 *apt unto*: ready for.

162 *chide*: scold me (for Tybalt's death).

162s.d. *offers*: starts.

166 *here . . . state*: your whole future
   depends on this.

168 *Or . . . hence*: Friar Lawrence offers
   another option.
   *from hence*: get away from here.
169 *Sojourn*: stay.
   *find . . . man*: keep in touch with your
   personal servant (Balthasar).
171 *Every . . . hap*: every piece of good
   fortune.
173 *calls . . . me*: calls me away.
174 *It . . . thee*: I would be sorry to leave
   you in such a hurry.

But look thou stay not till the Watch be set,
For then thou canst not pass to Mantua,
150 Where thou shalt live till we can find a time
To blaze your marriage, reconcile your friends,
Beg pardon of the prince, and call thee back
With twenty hundred thousand times more joy
Than thou went'st forth in lamentation.
155 Go before, Nurse, commend me to thy lady,
And bid her hasten all the house to bed,
Which heavy sorrow makes them apt unto.
Romeo is coming.

**Nurse**

O Lord, I could have stay'd here all the night
160 To hear good counsel. O, what learning is!
My lord, I'll tell my lady you will come.

**Romeo**

Do so, and bid my sweet prepare to chide.

Nurse *offers to go in, and turns again*

**Nurse**

Here, sir, a ring she bid me give you, sir.
Hie you, make haste, for it grows very late.

**Romeo**

165 How well my comfort is revived by this.       [*Exit* Nurse

**Friar Lawrence**

Go hence, good night, and here stands all your state:
Either be gone before the Watch be set,
Or by the break of day disguis'd from hence.
Sojourn in Mantua; I'll find out your man,
170 And he shall signify from time to time
Every good hap to you that chances here.
Give me thy hand, 'tis late. Farewell, good night.

**Romeo**

But that a joy past joy calls out on me,
It were a grief, so brief to part with thee:
175 Farewell.                                [*Exeunt*

**Act 3 Scene 4**
Juliet's father makes plans for his daughter
to marry Paris.

1 *fall'n out*: happened.

2 *move*: propose the matter to.

11 *mew'd . . . heaviness*: shut up (like a
moulting hawk) in her sorrow.

12 *I . . . tender*: I will risk making an
offer.

16 *son*: son-in-law (Capulet gives Paris an
honorary title).

17 *mark . . . me*: are you paying attention
to me.

18 *soft*: wait a minute.

23 *Well . . . ado*: we won't have any grand
affair, then; Capulet addresses his
wife—who is perhaps alarmed at the
short notice. Some editions read 'We'll
keep no great ado'.

24 *late*: recently.

25 *held him carelessly*: did not care very
much about him.

# SCENE 4

*Monday late evening*: Capulet's *house. Enter old*
Capulet, *his* Wife, *and* Paris

**Capulet**
Things have fall'n out, sir, so unluckily
That we have had no time to move our daughter.
Look you, she lov'd her kinsman Tybalt dearly,
And so did I. Well, we were born to die.
5   'Tis very late, she'll not come down tonight.
I promise you, but for your company,
I would have been abed an hour ago.
      **Paris**
These times of woe afford no times to woo.
Madam, good night, commend me to your daughter.
      **Lady Capulet**
10   I will, and know her mind early tomorrow;
Tonight she's mew'd up to her heaviness.

Paris *offers to go in, and* Capulet *calls him again*

**Capulet**
Sir Paris, I will make a desperate tender
Of my child's love: I think she will be rul'd
In all respects by me; nay more, I doubt it not.
15   Wife, go you to her ere you go to bed,
Acquaint her here of my son Paris' love,
And bid her—mark you me?—on Wednesday next—
But soft, what day is this?
      **Paris**
                                Monday my lord.
      **Capulet**
Monday, ha, ha! Well, Wednesday is too soon,
20   A' Thursday let it be—a' Thursday, tell her,
She shall be married to this noble earl.
Will you be ready? do you like this haste?
Well, keep no great ado—a friend or two,
For hark you, Tybalt being slain so late,
25   It may be thought we held him carelessly,

28 *there an end*: no more.

29 *I would*: I wish.

32 *against*: in time for.

34 *Afore me*: indeed (a mild
exclamation).
35 *by and by*: immediately.

**Act 3 Scene 5**
It is already dawn, and Romeo must leave
Juliet. Their parting is interrupted by the
Nurse, warning them that Juliet's mother is
approaching. Lady Capulet brings news of
the arranged marriage.

3 *fearful*: full of fear.

7 *envious*: malicious.
8 *severing*: parting.
9 *Night's candles*: the stars.

13 *meteor . . . exhal'd*: Meteors were
thought to be formed by vapours
drawn up ('exhaled') from the earth by
the sun, and then ignited.

17 *tane*: taken, caught.
18 *so thou*: if you.

Being our kinsman, if we revel much:
Therefore we'll have some half a dozen friends,
And there an end. But what say you to Thursday?
    **Paris**
My lord, I would that Thursday were tomorrow.
    **Capulet**
30 Well, get you gone, a'Thursday be it then.—
Go you to Juliet ere you go to bed,
Prepare her, wife, against this wedding day.
Farewell, my lord. Light to my chamber, ho!
Afore me, it is so very late that we
35 May call it early by and by. Good night.    [*Exeunt*

# Scene 5

*Very early Tuesday morning: Juliet's bedroom. Enter
Romeo and Juliet aloft as at the window*

    **Juliet**
Wilt thou be gone? It is not yet near day:
It was the nightingale, and not the lark,
That pierc'd the fearful hollow of thine ear;
Nightly she sings on yond pomegranate tree.
5 Believe me, love, it was the nightingale.
    **Romeo**
It was the lark, the herald of the morn,
No nightingale. Look, love, what envious streaks
Do lace the severing clouds in yonder east:
Night's candles are burnt out, and jocund day
10 Stands tiptoe on the misty mountain tops.
I must be gone and live, or stay and die.
    **Juliet**
Yond light is not daylight, I know it, I:
It is some meteor that the sun exhal'd
To be to thee this night a torch-bearer,
15 And light thee on thy way to Mantua.
Therefore stay yet, thou need'st not to be gone.
    **Romeo**
Let me be tane, let me be put to death,
I am content, so thou wilt have it so.

20 *reflex . . . brow*: reflection of the
   moon's face; 'Cynthia' is another
   name for the goddess of the moon.
21–2 *the lark . . . heads*: The lark sings
   when it is in flight.
22 *vaulty*: over-arching.
23 *care*: desire.
   *will*: wish.

28 *Straining*: forcing out.
   *sharps*: shrill notes of music.
29 *division*: separation; a musical term
   describing a rapid series of short,
   clear notes.
31 *Some . . . eyes*: Juliet refers to some
   belief that the toad's fine eyes had
   once belonged to the lark.
   *loathed*: loathèd.
32 *I would . . . too*: i.e. because an ugly
   croaking would be more appropriate to
   signal this morning.
33 *arm . . . affray*: scare us away from
   each other.
34 *hunt's-up*: A morning song to serenade
   a bride on the day after her wedding,
   or to call huntsmen to the field.

I'll say yon grey is not the morning's eye,
20 'Tis but the pale reflex of Cynthia's brow;
Nor that is not the lark whose notes do beat
The vaulty heaven so high above our heads.
I have more care to stay than will to go:
Come, death, and welcome! Juliet wills it so.
25 How is't, my soul? Let's talk, it is not day.
    **Juliet**
It is, it is, hie hence, be gone, away!
It is the lark that sings so out of tune,
Straining harsh discords and unpleasing sharps.
Some say the lark makes sweet division:
30 This doth not so, for she divideth us.
Some say the lark and loathed toad chang'd eyes;
O now I would they had chang'd voices too,
Since arm from arm that voice doth us affray,
Hunting thee hence with hunt's-up to the day.
35 O now be gone, more light and light it grows.
    **Romeo**
More light and light, more dark and dark our woes!

*Enter* Nurse *hastily*

    **Nurse**
Madam!
    **Juliet**
Nurse?
    **Nurse**
Your lady mother is coming to your chamber.
40 The day is broke, be wary, look about.            [*Exit*
    **Juliet**
Then, window, let day in, and let life out.
    **Romeo**
Farewell, farewell! one kiss, and I'll descend.

*He goeth down*

    **Juliet**
Art thou gone so, love, lord, ay husband, friend?
I must hear from thee every day in the hour,
45 For in a minute there are many days.

43 *friend*: lover.

45 *For . . . days*: because each minute
   seems like many days.

'I have more care to stay than will to go.' (*3*, 5, 23) Mark Rylance as Romeo and Georgia Slowe as Juliet, Royal Shakespeare Company, 1990.

46 *count*: way of reckoning.
*much in years*: very old.

O, by this count I shall be much in years
Ere I again behold my Romeo!
    **Romeo**
[*From below*] Farewell!
I will omit no opportunity
50 That may convey my greetings, love, to thee.
    **Juliet**
O think'st thou we shall ever meet again?
    **Romeo**
I doubt it not, and all these woes shall serve
For sweet discourses in our times to come.
    **Juliet**

54 *ill-divining*: foreboding, pessimistic.

55 *so low*: i.e. because Romeo has
climbed down from the balcony into
the orchard.

O God, I have an ill-divining soul!
55 Methinks I see thee now, thou art so low,
As one dead in the bottom of a tomb.
Either my eyesight fails, or thou look'st pale.
    **Romeo**
And trust me, love, in my eye so do you:
Dry sorrow drinks our blood. Adieu, adieu!    [*Exit*

59 *Dry*: thirsty; it was thought that every
sigh wasted a drop of the heart's
blood.

    **Juliet**
60 O Fortune, Fortune, all men call thee fickle;
If thou art fickle, what dost thou with him

61 *what dost thou*: why are you
concerned.

That is renown'd for faith? Be fickle, Fortune:
For then I hope thou wilt not keep him long,
But send him back.

*Enter mother, Lady Capulet, below*

    **Lady Capulet**
                Ho, daughter, are you up?
    **Juliet**
65 Who is't that calls? It is my lady mother.
Is she not down so late, or up so early?
What unaccustom'd cause procures her hither?

66 *Is . . . early*: is she very late going to
bed, or getting up very early.
67 *procures*: fetches.
67s.d. *She . . . below*: Only Q1 has this
stage direction; Juliet must come on
to the main acting area because her
father's rage needs space for
performance.
68 *how now*: what's the matter.

*She goeth down from the window and enters below*

    **Lady Capulet**
Why how now, Juliet?
    **Juliet**
                Madam, I am not well.

72 *have done*: stop crying.
72–3 *Some . . . wit*: a moderate grief shows much love, but excessive grief always shows lack of sense.
74 *such . . . loss*: a loss that I feel so much.

75 *feel . . . friend*: grieve for the loss to yourself rather than grieve for the friend you have lost—i.e. Tybalt.

76–7 *Feeling . . . friend*: because I feel the loss so much, I am forced to weep for the friend I have lost—i.e. Romeo.

81 *Villain . . . asunder*: Romeo is very far from being a villain; may Romeo never be called a villain.

83 *grieve*: distress; anger. Juliet's words, intended to mislead her mother, are deliberately ambiguous.

86 *Would*: I wish that.

88 *one*: someone I know.
89 *runagate*: fugitive wretch.
90 *unaccustom'd dram*: extraordinary little drink.

95 *vex'd*: troubled.

**Lady Capulet**
Evermore weeping for your cousin's death?
70 What, wilt thou wash him from his grave with tears?
And if thou couldst, thou couldst not make him live;
Therefore have done. Some grief shows much of love,
But much of grief shows still some want of wit.
    **Juliet**
Yet let me weep for such a feeling loss.
    **Lady Capulet**
75 So shall you feel the loss, but not the friend
Which you weep for.
    **Juliet**
                                Feeling so the loss,
I cannot choose but ever weep the friend.
    **Lady Capulet**
Well, girl, thou weep'st not so much for his death
As that the villain lives which slaughter'd him.
    **Juliet**
80 What villain, madam?
    **Lady Capulet**
                                That same villain Romeo.
    **Juliet**
[*Aside*] Villain and he be many miles asunder.—
God pardon him, I do with all my heart:
And yet no man like he doth grieve my heart.
    **Lady Capulet**
That is because the traitor murderer lives.
    **Juliet**
85 Ay, madam, from the reach of these my hands.
Would none but I might venge my cousin's death!
    **Lady Capulet**
We will have vengeance for it, fear thou not:
Then weep no more. I'll send to one in Mantua,
Where that same banish'd runagate doth live,
90 Shall give him such an unaccustom'd dram
That he shall soon keep Tybalt company;
And then I hope thou wilt be satisfied.
    **Juliet**
Indeed I never shall be satisfied
With Romeo, till I behold him—dead—
95 Is my poor heart, so for a kinsman vex'd.

96 *find out but*: only find out.

97 *temper*: mix.

101 *wreak*: avenge; bestow.

105 *needy*: unhappy.

107 *careful*: caring.

108 *heaviness*: sorrow.

109 *sorted out*: selected, appointed.
     *sudden*: speedy, surprising.
110 *look'd not for*: did not expect to see.

111 *in happy time*: how fortunate.

Madam, if you could find out but a man
To bear a poison, I would temper it,
That Romeo should upon receipt thereof
Soon sleep in quiet. O how my heart abhors
100 To hear him nam'd and cannot come to him,
To wreak the love I bore my cousin
Upon his body that hath slaughter'd him!
 **Lady Capulet**
Find thou the means, and I'll find such a man.
But now I'll tell thee joyful tidings, girl.
 **Juliet**
105 And joy comes well in such a needy time.
What are they, beseech your ladyship?
 **Lady Capulet**
Well, well, thou hast a careful father, child,
One who, to put thee from thy heaviness,
Hath sorted out a sudden day of joy,
110 That thou expects not, nor I look'd not for.
 **Juliet**
Madam, in happy time, what day is that?
 **Lady Capulet**
Marry, my child, early next Thursday morn,
The gallant, young, and noble gentleman,
The County Paris, at Saint Peter's Church,
115 Shall happily make thee there a joyful bride.
 **Juliet**
Now by Saint Peter's Church and Peter too,
He shall not make me there a joyful bride.
I wonder at this haste, that I must wed
Ere he that should be husband comes to woo.
120 I pray you tell my lord and father, madam,
I will not marry yet, and when I do, I swear
It shall be Romeo, whom you know I hate,
Rather than Paris. These are news indeed!
 **Lady Capulet**
Here comes your father, tell him so yourself;
125 And see how he will take it at your hands.

*Enter* Capulet *and* Nurse

**Capulet**
When the sun sets, the earth doth drizzle dew,
But for the sunset of my brother's son
It rains downright.
How now, a conduit, girl? What, still in tears?
130 Evermore show'ring? In one little body
Thou counterfeits a bark, a sea, a wind:
For still thy eyes, which I may call the sea,
Do ebb and flow with tears; the bark thy body is,
Sailing in this salt flood; the winds, thy sighs,
135 Who, raging with thy tears and they with them,
Without a sudden calm, will overset
Thy tempest-tossed body. How now, wife,
Have you deliver'd to her our decree?
**Lady Capulet**
Ay, sir, but she will none, she gives you thanks.
140 I would the fool were married to her grave.
**Capulet**
Soft, take me with you, take me with you, wife.
How, will she none? doth she not give us thanks?
Is she not proud? doth she not count her blest,
Unworthy as she is, that we have wrought
145 So worthy a gentleman to be her bride?
**Juliet**
Not proud you have, but thankful that you have:
Proud can I never be of what I hate,
But thankful even for hate that is meant love.
**Capulet**
How how, how how, chopt-logic? What is this?
150 'Proud', and 'I thank you', and 'I thank you not',
And yet 'not proud', mistress minion you?
Thank me no thankings, nor proud me no prouds,
But fettle your fine joints 'gainst Thursday next,
To go with Paris to Saint Peter's Church,
155 Or I will drag thee on a hurdle thither.
Out, you green-sickness carrion! out, you baggage!
You tallow-face!
**Lady Capulet**
                Fie, fie, what, are you mad?

128 *It . . . downright*: Capulet refers to the flood of tears from Juliet—but his show of sympathy quickly changes to anger.
129 *conduit*: fountain; these were sometimes made with human figures.
131 *thou counterfeits*: you imitate. *bark*: boat.
132 *still*: constantly.

136 *Without . . . calm*: unless you calm down quickly.
137 *tossed*: tossèd.
138 *decree*: decision.

139 *she . . . thanks*: she won't have anything to do with it, thank you very much (Lady Capulet is sarcastic).

141 *take . . . you*: let me understand you.

143 *proud*: honoured (with what is being done for her).
145 *bride*: i.e. bridegroom (the usage was already archaic in Shakespeare's time).
146 *Not . . . have*: not pleased with what has been done, but grateful to you for thinking of it.
148 *meant love*: intended as love.
149 *chopt-logic*: language-twisting, sophistical argument.
151 *mistress . . . you*: you spoiled little madam.
152 *Thank . . . prouds*: enough of these words 'thank' and 'proud'.
153 *fettle . . . joints*: get yourself ready (Capulet uses stable language). *'gainst*: in preparation for.
155 *hurdle*: wooden frame on which traitors were dragged through the streets to execution.
156-7 *Out . . . face*: Capulet's outrage struggles to find insults for Juliet, whose face is pale as wax ('tallow') with grief.
156 *green-sickness carrion*: anaemic lifeless corpse.

**Juliet**
Good father, I beseech you on my knees,
Hear me with patience but to speak a word.

*She kneels down*

**Capulet**
160 Hang thee, young baggage, disobedient wretch!
I tell thee what: get thee to church a'Thursday,
Or never after look me in the face.
Speak not, reply not, do not answer me!
My fingers itch. Wife, we scarce thought us blest
165 That God had lent us but this only child,
But now I see this one is one too much,
And that we have a curse in having her.
Out on her, hilding!
**Nurse**
                                    God in heaven bless her!
You are to blame, my lord, to rate her so.
**Capulet**
170 And why, my Lady Wisdom? Hold your tongue,
Good Prudence, smatter with your gossips, go.
**Nurse**
I speak no treason.
**Capulet**
                                    O God-i-goden!
**Nurse**
May not one speak?
**Capulet**
                                    Peace, you mumbling fool!
Utter your gravity o'er a gossip's bowl,
175 For here we need it not.
**Lady Capulet**
                                    You are too hot.
**Capulet**
God's bread, it makes me mad! Day, night, work, play,
Alone, in company, still my care hath been
To have her match'd; and having now provided
A gentleman of noble parentage,
180 Of fair demesnes, youthful and nobly lign'd,
Stuff'd, as they say, with honourable parts,

164 *itch*: i.e. to strike Juliet.

168 *hilding*: worthless creature.

169 *rate*: berate, scold.

171 *smatter*: chatter.
*gossips*: prattling old women.

172 *God-i-goden*: Good night!; an
expression of annoyance.

174 *gravity*: words of wisdom.
175 *hot*: passionate.

176 *God's bread*: by the body of God—i.e.
the bread consecrated at mass.
178 *match'd*: suitably married.
180 *demesnes*: inherited estates.
*nobly lign'd*: lineally descended from
noble ancestors.

181 *parts*: qualities.

183 *puling fool*: whimpering silly child.

184 *mammet*: doll, puppet.
*in . . . tender*: at the moment when
fortune offers her a gift.

188 *Graze . . . me*: go off anywhere you
like, you're not living here.
189 *I . . . jest*: I'm not in the habit of
making jokes.
190 *lay . . . advise*: think deeply and
consider it.

195 *be forsworn*: break my word.

200-1 *make . . . lies*: Juliet
(unconsciously) anticipates her
tragedy's outcome.

205-8 *My husband . . . earth*: Juliet's
marriage vow is registered in heaven,
and so long as Romeo is alive, she
cannot be released from it.

209 *practise stratagems*: play cruel tricks.

213 *all . . . nothing*: The Nurse is willing to
lay a bet.
214 *challenge you*: claim you as his wife.

Proportion'd as one's thought would wish a man,
And then to have a wretched puling fool,
A whining mammet, in her fortune's tender,
185 To answer 'I'll not wed, I cannot love;
I am too young, I pray you pardon me.'
But and you will not wed, I'll pardon you:
Graze where you will, you shall not house with me.
Look to't, think on't, I do not use to jest.
190 Thursday is near, lay hand on heart, advise:
And you be mine, I'll give you to my friend;
And you be not, hang, beg, starve, die in the streets,
For by my soul, I'll ne'er acknowledge thee,
Nor what is mine shall never do thee good.
195 Trust to't, bethink you, I'll not be forsworn.            [*Exit*
    **Juliet**
Is there no pity sitting in the clouds
That sees into the bottom of my grief?
O sweet my mother, cast me not away!
Delay this marriage for a month, a week,
200 Or if you do not, make the bridal bed
In that dim monument where Tybalt lies.
    **Lady Capulet**
Talk not to me, for I'll not speak a word.
Do as thou wilt, for I have done with thee.            [*Exit*
    **Juliet**
O God!—O Nurse, how shall this be prevented?
205 My husband is on earth, my faith in heaven;
How shall that faith return again to earth,
Unless that husband send it me from heaven
By leaving earth? Comfort me, counsel me.
Alack, alack, that heaven should practise stratagems
210 Upon so soft a subject as myself!
What say'st thou? hast thou not a word of joy?
Some comfort, Nurse.
    **Nurse**
                  Faith, here it is:
Romeo is banish'd, and all the world to nothing
That he dares ne'er come back to challenge you;
215 Or if he do, it needs must be by stealth.
Then since the case so stands as now it doth,
I think it best you married with the County.

O, he's a lovely gentleman!
Romeo's a dishclout to him. An eagle, madam,
220 Hath not so green, so quick, so fair an eye
As Paris hath. Beshrew my very heart,
I think you are happy in this second match,
For it excels your first, or if it did not,
Your first is dead, or 'twere as good he were
225 As living here and you no use of him.
        **Juliet**
Speak'st thou from thy heart?
        **Nurse**
And from my soul too, else beshrew them both.
        **Juliet**
Amen.
        **Nurse**
What?
        **Juliet**
230 Well, thou hast comforted me marvellous much.
Go in, and tell my lady I am gone,
Having displeas'd my father, to Lawrence' cell,
To make confession and to be absolv'd.
        **Nurse**
Marry, I will, and this is wisely done.              [*Exit*
        **Juliet**
235 [*She looks after* Nurse] Ancient damnation! O most
        wicked fiend!
Is it more sin to wish me thus forsworn,
Or to dispraise my lord with that same tongue
Which she hath prais'd him with above compare
So many thousand times? Go, counsellor,
240 Thou and my bosom henceforth shall be twain.
I'll to the Friar to know his remedy;
If all else fail, myself have power to die.              [*Exit*

219  *a dishclout to*: a dishrag by comparison with.

221  *Beshrew . . . heart*: curse my heart, indeed.
222  *happy*: fortunate.

228  *Amen*: so be it; Juliet endorses the Nurse's curse on her heart and soul.

235  *Ancient damnation*: damned old woman.

236  *sin*: sinful.

238  *above compare*: as being above comparison.

240  *bosom*: inmost secret thoughts. *twain*: two, separated; Juliet will no longer confide in her Nurse.
241  *I'll to*: I'll go to.
242  *myself . . . die*: I have the power to kill myself.

# ACT 4

## SCENE 1

*Tuesday morning:* Friar Lawrence's *cell. Enter* Friar Lawrence *and* County Paris

**Friar Lawrence**
On Thursday, sir? the time is very short.
**Paris**
My father Capulet will have it so,
And I am nothing slow to slack his haste.
**Friar Lawrence**
You say you do not know the lady's mind?
5 Uneven is the course, I like it not.
**Paris**
Immoderately she weeps for Tybalt's death,
And therefore have I little talk'd of love,
For Venus smiles not in a house of tears.
Now, sir, her father counts it dangerous
10 That she do give her sorrow so much sway;
And in his wisdom hastes our marriage
To stop the inundation of her tears,
Which too much minded by herself alone
May be put from her by society.
15 Now do you know the reason of this haste.
**Friar Lawrence**
[*Aside*] I would I knew not why it should be slow'd.—
Look, sir, here comes the lady toward my cell.

*Enter* Juliet

**Paris**
Happily met, my lady and my wife!
**Juliet**
That may be, sir, when I may be a wife.
**Paris**
20 That 'may be' must be, love, on Thursday next.

3 *nothing slow*: by no means reluctant. *slack*: lessen.

4 *mind*: opinion.

5 *Uneven . . . course*: it's a one-sided way of proceeding.

8 *Venus*: the goddess of love.

10 *sway*: scope.
11 *marriage*: The word must be pronounced with three syllables.
12 *inundation*: flooding.
13 *minded*: thought about.
14 *society*: companionship.

19 *That . . . wife*: Juliet's cool response to Paris marks a new development in her character.

**Juliet**

What must be shall be.

**Friar Lawrence**

That's a certain text.

**Paris**

Come you to make confession to this father?

**Juliet**

To answer that, I should confess to you.

**Paris**

Do not deny to him that you love me.

**Juliet**

25 I will confess to you that I love him.

**Paris**

So will ye, I am sure, that you love me.

**Juliet**

If I do so, it will be of more price,

Being spoke behind your back, than to your face.

**Paris**

Poor soul, thy face is much abus'd with tears.

**Juliet**

30 The tears have got small victory by that,

For it was bad enough before their spite.

**Paris**

Thou wrong'st it more than tears with that report.

**Juliet**

That is no slander, sir, which is a truth,

And what I spake, I spake it to my face.

**Paris**

35 Thy face is mine, and thou hast slander'd it.

**Juliet**

It may be so, for it is not mine own.

Are you at leisure, holy father, now,

Or shall I come to you at evening mass?

**Friar Lawrence**

My leisure serves me, pensive daughter, now.

40 My lord, we must entreat the time alone.

**Paris**

God shield I should disturb devotion!

Juliet, on Thursday early will I rouse ye;

Till then adieu, and keep this holy kiss.                    [ *Exit*

25  *love him*: i.e. Romeo.

26  *will ye*: you will confess to the friar.

27  *more price*: greater worth.

34  *to my face*: (a) openly; (b) about my face.

39  *My . . . me*: I am free.
    *pensive*: sad, thoughtful.
40  *entreat . . . alone*: ask to be alone for the present.
41  *shield*: forbid.
42  *early . . . ye*: The Elizabethan wedding-day started when the bridegroom woke his bride with music, and led her to the church.

**Juliet**
O shut the door, and when thou hast done so,
45 Come weep with me, past hope, past cure, past help!
    **Friar Lawrence**
O Juliet, I already know thy grief,
It strains me past the compass of my wits.
I hear thou must, and nothing may prorogue it,
On Thursday next be married to this County.
    **Juliet**
50 Tell me not, Friar, that thou hearest of this,
Unless thou tell me how I may prevent it.
If in thy wisdom thou canst give no help,
Do thou but call my resolution wise,
And with this knife I'll help it presently.
55 God join'd my heart and Romeo's, thou our hands,
And ere this hand, by thee to Romeo's seal'd,
Shall be the label to another deed,
Or my true heart with treacherous revolt
Turn to another, this shall slay them both:
60 Therefore, out of thy long-experienc'd time,
Give me some present counsel, or, behold,
'Twixt my extremes and me this bloody knife
Shall play the umpire, arbitrating that
Which the commission of thy years and art
65 Could to no issue of true honour bring.
Be not so long to speak, I long to die,
If what thou speak'st speak not of remedy.
    **Friar Lawrence**
Hold, daughter, I do spy a kind of hope,
Which craves as desperate an execution
70 As that is desperate which we would prevent.
If, rather than to marry County Paris,
Thou hast the strength of will to slay thyself,
Then it is likely thou wilt undertake
A thing like death to chide away this shame,
75 That cop'st with Death himself to scape from it;
And if thou dar'st, I'll give thee remedy.
    **Juliet**
O bid me leap, rather than marry Paris,
From off the battlements of any tower,
Or walk in thievish ways, or bid me lurk

---

47 *strains*: perplexes.
*compass of my wits*: limits of my mind.
48 *prorogue*: postpone.

53 *resolution*: decision.
54 *presently*: immediately.

57 *label*: the wax seal fastened to a document ('deed') to make it legal.

59 *both*: i.e. her hand and her heart.
60 *long-experienc'd time*: age and experience.
61 *present counsel*: advice at once.
62 *extremes*: desperate straits.
*bloody*: capable of shedding blood.
63 *arbitrating that*: resolving that problem.
64 *commission*: authority.
*art*: skill.
65 *issue of true honour*: honourable solution.
66 *long*: slow.

69–70 *craves . . . prevent*: demands an action as drastic as the threat that we are trying to prevent.

74 *chide*: drive.
75 *That . . . himself*: since you are willing to deal with death itself.

79 *thievish ways*: lanes frequented by thieves.
*lurk*: linger.

81 *charnel-house*: the repository for
  bones dug up in the course of digging
  new graves in the churchyard.
83 *reeky*: stinking.
  *chapless*: jawless (the bottom of the
  jaw would be knocked off with the
  spade).

91 *look*: see to it.
  *lie*: sleep.

93 *vial*: small bottle.
94 *distilling liquor*: liquid which will
  infuse the whole body (as the Friar
  explains).
96 *a cold . . . humour*: a cold, drowsy
  sensation.
97 *native progress*: natural movement.
  *surcease*: stop.

100 *to wanny ashes*: to become as pale as
  ashes.
  *eyes' windows*: eyelids.
102 *supple government*: power of
  movement.

104 *borrow'd*: false.
109 *manner*: fashion.
110 *uncover'd*: with face uncovered
  (probably because—in the eyes of
  society—she was not married).

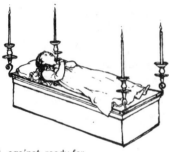

113 *against*: ready for.
114 *drift*: plan.

80 Where serpents are; chain me with roaring bears,
   Or hide me nightly in a charnel-house,
   O'ercover'd quite with dead men's rattling bones,
   With reeky shanks and yellow chapless skulls;
   Or bid me go into a new-made grave,
85 And hide me with a dead man in his shroud—
   Things that to hear them told have made me tremble—
   And I will do it without fear or doubt,
   To live an unstain'd wife to my sweet love.
       **Friar Lawrence**
   Hold then, go home, be merry, give consent
90 To marry Paris. Wednesday is tomorrow;
   Tomorrow night look that thou lie alone,
   Let not the Nurse lie with thee in thy chamber.
   Take thou this vial, being then in bed,
   And this distilling liquor drink thou off,
95 When presently through all thy veins shall run
   A cold and drowsy humour; for no pulse
   Shall keep his native progress, but surcease;
   No warmth, no breath shall testify thou livest;
   The roses in thy lips and cheeks shall fade
100 To wanny ashes, thy eyes' windows fall,
   Like Death when he shuts up the day of life;
   Each part, depriv'd of supple government,
   Shall stiff and stark and cold appear like death,
   And in this borrow'd likeness of shrunk death
105 Thou shalt continue two and forty hours,
   And then awake as from a pleasant sleep.
   Now when the bridegroom in the morning comes
   To rouse thee from thy bed, there art thou dead.
   Then as the manner of our country is,
110 In thy best robes, uncover'd on the bier,
   Thou shall be borne to that same ancient vault
   Where all the kindred of the Capulets lie.
   In the mean time, against thou shalt awake,
   Shall Romeo by my letters know our drift,
115 And hither shall he come, and he and I
   Will watch thy waking, and that very night
   Shall Romeo bear thee hence to Mantua.
   And this shall free thee from this present shame,

119 *inconstant toy*: irresolute fancy.

120 *Abate*: weaken.

122 *Hold*: here it is.

125 *help afford*: give help.

**Act 4 Scene 2**
The Capulets are preparing for the wedding; Juliet promises her father that she will obey him—and the wedding day is changed.

1 *writ*: written.

2 *cunning*: skilful.

3 *none ill*: no bad ones.
*try*: test.
6–7 *'tis . . . fingers*: The saying is proverbial: a good cook will approve his cooking by tasting it.

10 *unfurnish'd*: unprepared.

14 *harlotry*: silly little hussy.

If no inconstant toy, nor womanish fear,
120 Abate thy valour in the acting it.
    **Juliet**
Give me, give me! O tell not me of fear.
    **Friar Lawrence**
Hold, get you gone, be strong and prosperous
In this resolve; I'll send a friar with speed
To Mantua, with my letters to thy lord.
    **Juliet**
125 Love give me strength, and strength shall help afford.
Farewell, dear father.         [*Exeunt*

# SCENE 2

*Tuesday afternoon:* Capulet's *house. Enter father,* Capulet, *mother,* Lady Capulet, Nurse *and* Servingmen, *two or three*

    **Capulet**
So many guests invite as here are writ.
                    [*Exit* Servingman
Sirrah, go hire me twenty cunning cooks.
    **Servingman**
You shall have none ill, sir, for I'll try if they can lick their fingers.
    **Capulet**
5 How canst thou try them so?
    **Servingman**
Marry, sir, 'tis an ill cook that cannot lick his own fingers; therefore he that cannot lick his fingers goes not with me.
    **Capulet**
Go, be gone.            [*Exit* Servingman
10 We shall be much unfurnish'd for this time.
What, is my daughter gone to Friar Lawrence?
    **Nurse**
Ay forsooth.
    **Capulet**
Well, he may chance to do some good on her.
A peevish self-will'd harlotry it is.

*Enter* Juliet

**Nurse**

15   *shrift*: confession.

15   See where she comes from shrift with merry look.
    **Capulet**

16   *headstrong*: stubborn one.

How now, my headstrong, where have you been
    gadding?
    **Juliet**
Where I have learnt me to repent the sin
Of disobedient opposition

19   *behests*: demands.
    *enjoin'd*: instructed.

To you and your behests, and am enjoin'd
20   By holy Lawrence to fall prostrate here
To beg your pardon.

*She kneels down*

              Pardon, I beseech you!

22   *I am ever rul'd*: I always will be ruled.

Henceforward I am ever rul'd by you.
    **Capulet**
Send for the County, go tell him of this.
I'll have this knot knit up tomorrow morning.
    **Juliet**

24   *tomorrow morning*: Delighted by Juliet's submission, Capulet changes the marriage day to Wednesday—which will have disastrous results.
26   *becomed*: becomèd; appropriate, befitting.

25   I met the youthful lord at Lawrence' cell,
And gave him what becomed love I might,
Not stepping o'er the bounds of modesty.
    **Capulet**
Why, I am glad on't, this is well, stand up.
This is as't should be. Let me see the County;
30   Ay, marry, go, I say, and fetch him hither.
Now afore God, this reverend holy Friar,

32   *bound*: indebted.

All our whole city is much bound to him.
    **Juliet**

33   *closet*: private room.
34   *sort*: choose.

Nurse, will you go with me into my closet,
To help me sort such needful ornaments

35   *furnish*: equip.

35   As you think fit to furnish me tomorrow?
    **Lady Capulet**
No, not till Thursday, there is time enough.
    **Capulet**
Go, Nurse, go with her, we'll to church tomorrow.
             [*Exeunt* Juliet *and* Nurse

38 *short . . . provision*: not have enough food ready.

39 *near night*: Shakespeare is accelerating the progress of the play; Juliet, who visited Friar Lawrence in the morning, has only just returned.

41 *deck*: dress.

42 *let me alone*: leave me to myself.

43 *huswife*: housewife (pronounced 'húsif').

44 *forth*: out of the house.

46 *Against*: in preparation for.

47 *reclaim'd*: brought back to obedience.

**Act 4 Scene 3**
Although she is frightened, Juliet takes the Friar's drug.

1 *attires*: clothes.

3 *orisons*: prayers.

4 *state*: spiritual condition.

5 *cross*: contrary to my desires, stubborn.

7 *cull'd*: picked out.

8 *behoveful*: needful, fitting. *state*: social position.

12 *business*: The word must be pronounced with three syllables.

**Lady Capulet**
We shall be short in our provision,
'Tis now near night.
    **Capulet**
                    Tush, I will stir about,
40 And all things shall be well, I warrant thee, wife:
Go thou to Juliet, help to deck up her;
I'll not to bed tonight; let me alone,
I'll play the huswife for this once. What ho!
They are all forth. Well, I will walk myself
45 To County Paris, to prepare up him
Against tomorrow. My heart is wondrous light,
Since this same wayward girl is so reclaim'd.    [*Exeunt*

## SCENE 3

*Tuesday night*: Juliet's *bedroom. Enter* Juliet *and* Nurse

**Juliet**
Ay, those attires are best, but, gentle Nurse,
I pray thee leave me to myself tonight:
For I have need of many orisons
To move the heavens to smile upon my state,
5 Which, well thou knowest, is cross and full of sin.

*Enter mother,* Lady Capulet

**Lady Capulet**
What, are you busy, ho? need you my help?
    **Juliet**
No, madam, we have cull'd such necessaries
As are behoveful for our state tomorrow.
So please you, let me now be left alone,
10 And let the Nurse this night sit up with you,
For I am sure you have your hands full all,
In this so sudden business.
    **Lady Capulet**
                    Good night.
Get thee to bed and rest, for thou hast need.
        [*Exeunt* Lady Capulet *and* Nurse

**Juliet**

Farewell! God knows when we shall meet again.

15 I have a faint cold fear thrills through my veins
That almost freezes up the heat of life:
I'll call them back again to comfort me.
Nurse!—What should she do here?
My dismal scene I needs must act alone.

20 Come, vial.
What if this mixture do not work at all?
Shall I be married then tomorrow morning?
No, no, this shall forbid it; lie thou there.

*Laying down her dagger*

What if it be a poison which the Friar

25 Subtly hath minister'd to have me dead,
Lest in this marriage he should be dishonour'd,
Because he married me before to Romeo?
I fear it is, and yet methinks it should not,
For he hath still been tried a holy man.

30 How if, when I am laid into the tomb,
I wake before the time that Romeo
Come to redeem me? There's a fearful point!
Shall I not then be stifl'd in the vault,
To whose foul mouth no healthsome air breathes in,

35 And there die strangl'd ere my Romeo comes?
Or if I live, is it not very like
The horrible conceit of death and night,
Together with the terror of the place—
As in a vault, an ancient receptacle,

40 Where for this many hundred years the bones
Of all my buried ancestors are pack'd,
Where bloody Tybalt, yet but green in earth,
Lies fest'ring in his shroud, where, as they say,
At some hours in the night spirits resort—

45 Alack, alack, is it not like that I,
So early waking—what with loathsome smells,
And shrieks like mandrakes' torn out of the earth,
That living mortals hearing them run mad—
O, if I wake, shall I not be distraught,

50 Environed with all these hideous fears,

15 *faint cold fear*: fear causing faintness and coldness (see Extracts, from *Romeus and Juliet*, page 122). *thrills*: shivers.

19 *dismal*: dreadful.

23 *this*: i.e. the dagger.
25 *Subtly*: cunningly, deceitfully. *minister'd*: provided, prescribed.
29 *still been tried*: always been found.

32 *redeem*: rescue.

34 *healthsome*: wholesome, healthy.

37 *conceit of*: thoughts produced by.

39 *As*: as being.

42 *yet*: still. *but green in earth*: recently buried.

47 *mandrakes*: plants which were said to scream, causing madness or death, when their forked, man-shaped roots were pulled out of the ground.
50 *Environed*: environèd.

And madly play with my forefathers' joints,
And pluck the mangl'd Tybalt from his shroud,
And in this rage, with some great kinsman's bone,
As with a club, dash out my desp'rate brains?
55 O look! methinks I see my cousin's ghost
Seeking out Romeo that did spit his body
Upon a rapier's point. Stay, Tybalt, stay!
Romeo, Romeo, Romeo! Here's drink—I drink to thee.

*She falls upon her bed, within the curtains*

53 *rage*: frenzy.
56 *spit*: pierce.
57 *Stay*: stop.
58s.d. *within the curtains*: This stage direction (from Q1) shows that the bed was positioned on the 'inner stage' where it could be concealed by curtains.

## SCENE 4

*Early Wednesday morning:* Capulet's house. Enter *lady of the house,* Lady Capulet *and* Nurse *with herbs*

**Lady Capulet**
Hold, take these keys and fetch more spices, Nurse.
**Nurse**
They call for dates and quinces in the pastry.

*Enter old* Capulet

**Capulet**
Come, stir, stir, stir! the second cock hath crow'd,
The curfew bell hath rung, 'tis three a'clock.
5 Look to the bak'd meats, good Angelica,
Spare not for cost.
**Nurse**
                          Go, you cot-quean, go,
Get you to bed. Faith, you'll be sick tomorrow
For this night's watching.
**Capulet**
No, not a whit. What, I have watch'd ere now
10 All night for lesser cause, and ne'er been sick.
**Lady Capulet**
Ay, you have been a mouse-hunt in your time,
But I will watch you from such watching now.
                          [*Exeunt* Lady Capulet *and* Nurse

**Act 4 Scene 4**
The Capulet household prepares for the wedding, and the Nurse goes to wake Juliet.

2 *pastry*: the room where pie paste was prepared.

3 *second cock*: The cock was thought to crow at midnight, at 3 a.m., and just before dawn.
4 *curfew bell*: This was rung in the evening when the Watch was set (see 3, 3, 148), and again in the morning.
5 *Angelica*: perhaps a teasing name for the Nurse.
6 *spare not for cost*: don't think about the expense.
*cot-quean*: man who interferes in the woman's job (i.e. housework).
8 *watching*: keeping awake.
9 *whit*: bit.

11 *mouse-hunt*: woman-chaser.
12 *watch*: prevent.

13 *hood*: woman.

13s.d.  *spits*: iron bars for roasting meat over a fire.

**Capulet**
A jealous hood, a jealous hood!

*Enter three or four* Servingmen *with spits and logs and baskets*

                         Now, fellow,
What is there?
    **First Servingman**
15 Things for the cook, sir, but I know not what.
    **Capulet**
Make haste, make haste.         [*Exit* First Servingman
                Sirrah, fetch drier logs.
Call Peter, he will show thee where they are.
    **Second Servingman**
I have a head, sir, that will find out logs,
And never trouble Peter for the matter.
    **Capulet**
20 Mass, and well said, a merry whoreson, ha!
Thou shalt be loggerhead.
        [*Exeunt* Second Servingman *and any others*
                Good faith, 'tis day.
The County will be here with music straight,
For so he said he would.

*Play music within*

                I hear him near.
Nurse! Wife! What ho! What, Nurse, I say!

*Enter* Nurse

20 *Mass*: by the mass.
   *whoreson*: bastard.
21 *loggerhead*: (a) head of the logging party; (b) blockhead.
21s.d.  *any others*: The writer could not be certain how many actors would be available to swell the number of Servants.
22 *straight*: immediately.

25 *trim*: dress.

25 Go waken Juliet, go and trim her up,
I'll go and chat with Paris. Hie, make haste,
Make haste, the bridegroom he is come already,
Make haste, I say.               [*Exit*

**Act 4 Scene 5**
Juliet cannot be woken, and the whole family lament her death.

# Scene 5

*Juliet's bedroom*

**Nurse**
Mistress, what mistress! Juliet! Fast, I warrant her, she.
Why, lamb! why, lady! fie, you slug-a-bed!
Why, love, I say! madam! sweet heart! why, bride!
What, not a word? You take your pennyworths now;
5 Sleep for a week, for the next night I warrant
The County Paris hath set up his rest
That you shall rest but little. God forgive me!
Marry and amen! How sound is she asleep!
I needs must wake her. Madam, madam, madam!
10 Ay, let the County take you in your bed,
He'll fright you up, i'faith. Will it not be?

*Draws back the curtains*

What, dress'd, and in your clothes, and down again?
I must needs wake you. Lady, lady, lady!
Alas, alas! Help, help! my lady's dead!
15 O weraday that ever I was born!
Some aqua-vitae, ho! My lord! My lady!

*Enter mother, Lady Capulet*

**Lady Capulet**
What noise is here?
**Nurse**
            O lamentable day!
**Lady Capulet**
What is the matter?
**Nurse**
            Look, look! O heavy day!
**Lady Capulet**
O me, O me, my child, my only life!
20 Revive, look up, or I will die with thee.
Help, help! Call help.

*Enter father, Capulet*

1 *Fast*: fast asleep.
2 *slug-a-bed*: lazy person.

4 *pennyworths*: what little you can get.

6 *set up his rest*: made up his mind.

10 *take*: find.
11 *fright you up*: frighten you into getting up.

12 *down again*: lying down again (i.e. having got dressed).

**Capulet**

For shame, bring Juliet forth, her lord is come.

**Nurse**

She's dead, deceas'd, she's dead, alack the day!

**Lady Capulet**

Alack the day, she's dead, she's dead, she's dead!

**Capulet**

25 Hah, let me see her. Out alas, she's cold,

Her blood is settled, and her joints are stiff:

Life and these lips have long been separated;

Death lies on her like an untimely frost

Upon the sweetest flower of all the field.

**Nurse**

30 O lamentable day!

**Lady Capulet**

       O woeful time!

**Capulet**

Death that hath tane her hence to make me wail

Ties up my tongue and will not let me speak.

*Enter* Friar Lawrence *and the* County Paris *with the* Musicians

**Friar Lawrence**

Come, is the bride ready to go to church?

**Capulet**

Ready to go, but never to return.—

35 O son, the night before thy wedding day

Hath Death lain with thy wife. There she lies,

Flower as she was, deflowered by him.

Death is my son-in-law, Death is my heir,

My daughter he hath wedded. I will die,

40 And leave him all; life, living, all is Death's.

**Paris**

Have I thought long to see this morning's face,

And doth it give me such a sight as this?

**Lady Capulet**

Accurs'd, unhappy, wretched, hateful day!

Most miserable hour that e'er time saw

45 In lasting labour of his pilgrimage!

But one, poor one, one poor and loving child,

26 *is settled*: has ceased to flow.

28 *untimely*: early.

37 *deflowered*: deflowerèd.

40 *living*: property.

41 *thought long*: waited for a long time.
*this morning's face*: the dawn of this day.

45 *lasting*: everlasting.
*pilgrimage*: progress (from year to year).

47 *solace*: find solace.

But one thing to rejoice and solace in,
And cruel Death hath catch'd it from my sight!
    **Nurse**
O woe! O woeful, woeful, woeful day!
50 Most lamentable day, most woeful day
That ever, ever, I did yet behold!
O day, O day, O day, O hateful day!
Never was seen so black a day as this.
O woeful day, O woeful day!
    **Paris**

55 *divorced, wronged*: divorcèd, wrongèd.

55 Beguil'd, divorced, wronged, spited, slain!
Most detestable Death, by thee beguil'd,
By cruel, cruel thee quite overthrown!

58 *love in death*: my love even in death.

O love! O life! not life, but love in death!
    **Capulet**

59 *distressed*: distressèd.
60 *Uncomfortable*: grievous.
61 *solemnity*: ceremony.

Despis'd, distressed, hated, martyr'd, kill'd!
60 Uncomfortable time, why cam'st thou now
To murder, murder our solemnity?
O child, O child! my soul, and not my child!
Dead art thou. Alack, my child is dead,

64 *buried*: burièd.

And with my child my joys are buried.
    **Friar Lawrence**

65–6 *Confusion's cure . . . confusions*: the remedy for this disaster is not to be found in these outcries; the Friar throws cold water on the hysteria with his word-play.
67 *Had part*: shared.
79 *rosemary*: the herb of remembrance, worn at weddings and funerals.

65 Peace ho, for shame! Confusion's cure lives not
In these confusions. Heaven and yourself
Had part in this fair maid, now heaven hath all,
And all the better is it for the maid:
Your part in her you could not keep from death,
70 But heaven keeps his part in eternal life.
The most you sought was her promotion,
For 'twas your heaven she should be advanc'd,
And weep ye now, seeing she is advanc'd
Above the clouds, as high as heaven itself?
75 O, in this love, you love your child so ill
That you run mad, seeing that she is well.
She's not well married that lives married long,
But she's best married that dies married young.
Dry up your tears, and stick your rosemary

80 *corse*: corpse.
82 *fond nature*: foolish human nature.
83 *reason's merriment*: (Christian) reason should laugh at human weakness because death opens the way to everlasting life: 'to die is gain' (Philippians 1:21).

80 On this fair corse, and as the custom is,
And in her best array, bear her to church;
For though fond nature bids us all lament,
Yet nature's tears are reason's merriment.

**Capulet**

All things that we ordained festival,

85 Turn from their office to black funeral:

Our instruments to melancholy bells,

Our wedding cheer to sad burial feast;

Our solemn hymns to sullen dirges change;

Our bridal flowers serve for a buried corse;

90 And all things change them to the contrary.

**Friar Lawrence**

Sir, go you in, and, madam, go with him,

And go, Sir Paris. Every one prepare

To follow this fair corse unto her grave.

The heavens do low'r upon you for some ill;

95 Move them no more by crossing their high will.

*They all, but the* Nurse *and the* Musicians, *go forth,*
*casting rosemary on her, and shutting the curtains*

**First Musician**

Faith, we may put up our pipes and be gone.

**Nurse**

Honest good fellows, ah put up, put up,

For well you know this is a pitiful case.          [*Exit*

**First Musician**

Ay, by my troth, the case may be amended.

*Enter* Peter

**Peter**

100 Musicians, O musicians, 'Heart's ease', 'Heart's ease'! O,

and you will have me live, play 'Heart's ease'.

**First Musician**

Why 'Heart's ease'?

**Peter**

O musicians, because my heart itself plays 'My heart is

full'. O play me some merry dump to comfort me.

**Musicians**

105 Not a dump we, 'tis no time to play now.

**Peter**

You will not then?

---

**84** *ordained festival*: ordainèd; intended to be festive.
**85** *office*: function.

**87** *cheer*: banquet.

**90** *contrary*: opposite.

**94** *low'r*: frown.
**95** *Move*: anger.
    *crossing*: frustrating.

**96** *put up*: put away (in their cases).

**98** *pitiful case*: sorrowful state of affairs.

**99** *case*: the Musician speaks as though the Nurse refers to his instrument case.

**103–4** *'My heart is full'*: the first line of a popular song.
**104** *dump*: sad tune (a 'merry dump' would be impossible).

108 *soundly*: thoroughly.

110 *gleek*: gesture of scorn.
    *give you*: call you.
111 *minstrel*: a term of contempt (see
    3, 1, 43).
112 *serving-creature*: slave.

114 *pate*: head.
    *crotchets*: (a) musical notes;
    (b) strange ideas.
    *re . . . fa*: notes on the musical scale.
115 *note*: take notice of.
117 *And*: if.
117 *put . . . wit*: put your dagger away and
    show some sense.

118 *have at you*: I attack you.
    *dry-beat*: beat without drawing blood.

121–3 *When . . . sound*: The opening lines
    of a lyric 'In commendation of Music',
    by Richard Edwardes (1523–66).

**First Musician**
No.
**Peter**
I will then give it you soundly.
**First Musician**
What will you give us?
**Peter**
110 No money, on my faith, but the gleek; I will give you the
minstrel.
**First Musician**
Then will I give you the serving-creature.
**Peter**
Then will I lay the serving-creature's dagger on your
pate. I will carry no crotchets, I'll re you, I'll fa you. Do
115 you note me?
**First Musician**
And you re us and fa us, you note us.
**Second Musician**
Pray you put up your dagger, and put out your wit.
**Peter**
Then have at you with my wit! I will dry-beat you with
an iron wit, and put up my iron dagger. Answer me like
120 men:
　　　'When griping griefs the heart doth wound,
　　　And doleful dumps the mind oppress,
　　　Then music with her silver sound—'

125 *Catling*: the string of a small lute.

127 *Prates*: nonsense (literally, 'he
    chatters').
    *Rebeck*: a kind of fiddle.
128 *sound for*: play for.

129 *Soundpost*: wooden peg fixed below
    the bridge of a violin.

131 *I cry . . . singer*: I beg your pardon for
    asking a 'singer' to speak.
    *say*: speak.

135 *redress*: comfort.

137 *Jack*: scoundrel.
    *tarry*: wait for.
138 *stay dinner*: stay to dinner.

Why 'silver sound'? why 'music with her silver sound'?
125 What say you Simon Catling?
          **First Musician**
Marry, sir, because silver hath a sweet sound.
          **Peter**
Prates! What say you, Hugh Rebeck?
          **Second Musician**
I say 'silver sound' because musicians sound for silver.
          **Peter**
Prates too! What say you, James Soundpost?
          **Third Musician**
130 Faith, I know not what to say.
          **Peter**
O, I cry you mercy, you are the singer; I will say for you:
It is 'music with her silver sound' because musicians
have no gold for sounding.
          'Then music with her silver sound
135          With speedy help doth lend redress.'          [*Exit*
          **First Musician**
What a pestilent knave is this same!
          **Second Musician**
Hang him, Jack! Come, we'll in here, tarry for the
mourners, and stay dinner.          [*Exeunt*

# ACT 5

**Act 5 Scene 1**
Romeo is told that Juliet is dead.

## SCENE 1

*Wednesday morning: Mantua. Enter* Romeo

**Romeo**

1 *flattering truth*: wish-fulfilment;
 morning dreams were proverbially
 believed to be truthful.
2 *presage*: foretell.
 *at hand*: close by.
3 *My bosom's lord*: love.
 *throne*: Romeo's heart.
4 *spirit*: cheerfulness.

If I may trust the flattering truth of sleep,
My dreams presage some joyful news at hand.
My bosom's lord sits lightly in his throne,
And all this day an unaccustom'd spirit
5 Lifts me above the ground with cheerful thoughts.
I dreamt my lady came and found me dead
(Strange dream that gives a dead man leave to think!),
And breath'd such life with kisses in my lips
That I reviv'd and was an emperor.
10 Ah me, how sweet is love itself possess'd,
When but love's shadows are so rich in joy!

11 *but love's shadows*: the mere shadows
 (dreams) of love.

11s.d. *booted*: i.e. to show that he has
 just been travelling.

*Enter* Romeo's *man* Balthasar, *booted*

News from Verona! How now, Balthasar?
Dost thou not bring me letters from the Friar?
How doth my lady! Is my father well?
15 How doth my Juliet? That I ask again,
For nothing can be ill if she be well.

**Balthasar**

Then she is well and nothing can be ill:
Her body sleeps in Capels' monument,
And her immortal part with angels lives.
20 I saw her laid low in her kindred's vault,
And presently took post to tell it you.
O pardon me for bringing these ill news,
Since you did leave it for my office, sir.

18 *Capels'*: Capulets'.

21 *presently . . . post*: immediately set
 out, using post-horses (which were
 changed at inns along the route).
23 *office*: duty.

**Romeo**

Is it e'en so? then I defy you, stars!
25 Thou knowest my lodging, get me ink and paper,
And hire post-horses; I will hence tonight.

24 *e'en*: even, indeed.

28 *import*: threaten.

**Balthasar**
I do beseech you, sir, have patience:
Your looks are pale and wild, and do import
Some misadventure.
　　**Romeo**
　　　　　　　　　Tush, thou art deceiv'd.
30 Leave me, and do the thing I bid thee do.
Hast thou no letters to me from the Friar?
　　**Balthasar**
No, my good lord.
　　**Romeo**
　　　　　　　　No matter, get thee gone,
And hire those horses; I'll be with thee straight.
　　　　　　　　　　　　　　[*Exit* Balthasar
Well, Juliet, I will lie with thee tonight.

35 *Let's . . . means*: let me think what I
can use.

35 Let's see for means. O mischief, thou art swift
To enter in the thoughts of desperate men!
I do remember an apothecary,

38 *late*: recently.
*noted*: noticed.
39 *weeds*: clothes.
*overwhelming*: overhanging.
40 *Culling of simples*: gathering herbs.

And hereabouts 'a dwells, which late I noted
In tatter'd weeds, with overwhelming brows,
40 Culling of simples; meagre were his looks,
Sharp misery had worn him to the bones;
And in his needy shop a tortoise hung,
An alligator stuff'd, and other skins
Of ill-shap'd fishes, and about his shelves

45 *account*: number.
46 *earthen*: earthenware.
*bladders*: used for storing liquids.
47 *packthread*: strong string.
*cakes of roses*: rose petals
compressed into cakes and used as
perfumes.

45 A beggarly account of empty boxes,
Green earthen pots, bladders, and musty seeds,
Remnants of packthread, and old cakes of roses
Were thinly scatter'd, to make up a show.
Noting this penury, to myself I said,

51 *present death*: punishable by instant
death.
52 *caitiff*: miserable.
53 *forerun*: anticipate.

50 'And if a man did need a poison now,
Whose sale is present death in Mantua,
Here lives a caitiff wretch would sell it him.'
O this same thought did but forerun my need,
And this same needy man must sell it me.
55 As I remember, this should be the house.
Being holiday, the beggar's shop is shut.
What ho, apothecary!

'Put this in any liquid thing you will', (5, 1, 77). Zubin Varla as Romeo and Jeffery Dench as the Apothecary, Royal Shakespeare Company, 1995.

*Enter* Apothecary

**Apothecary**

                          Who calls so loud?

**Romeo**

Come hither, man. I see that thou art poor.

Hold, there is forty ducats; let me have

60  A dram of poison, such soon-speeding gear

As will disperse itself through all the veins,

That the life-weary taker may fall dead,

And that the trunk may be discharg'd of breath

As violently as hasty powder fir'd

65  Doth hurry from the fatal cannon's womb.

**Apothecary**

Such mortal drugs I have, but Mantua's law

Is death to any he that utters them.

**Romeo**

Art thou so bare and full of wretchedness,

And fearest to die? Famine is in thy cheeks,

70  Need and oppression starveth in thy eyes,

Contempt and beggary hangs upon thy back;

The world is not thy friend, nor the world's law,

The world affords no law to make thee rich;

59 *forty ducats*: gold coins; 'forty' would be a substantial sum.
60 *soon-speeding*: quick acting.
    *gear*: stuff.

63 *trunk*: body.
64 *fir'd*: when it is set on fire.

66 *mortal*: lethal.
67 *utters*: dispenses, offers for sale.

70 *oppression*: distress.
    *starveth in thine eyes*: show in the hungry look in your eyes.
71 *Contempt and beggary*: despised poverty.
    *hangs upon thy back*: i.e. with his clothes.

74  *it*: the law.

79  *dispatch*: kill.

84  *get . . . flesh*: grow fat.

85  *cordial*: a restorative medicine for the
    heart.

**Act 5 Scene 2**
Friar Lawrence, learning that Romeo has
not received his letter, hurries to the
Capulets' vault.

4  *his mind be writ*: he has written down
   his thoughts.

5  *barefoot brother*: i.e. another
   Franciscan friar; members of the
   Order always travelled barefoot, and in
   pairs.
6  *associate*: accompany.
8  *searchers of the town*: the town's
   health officers, whose duty was to
   view dead bodies and report on the
   cause of death.
10  *infectious pestilence*: plague.

Then be not poor, but break it and take this.
  **Apothecary**
75  My poverty, but not my will, consents.
  **Romeo**
I pay thy poverty and not thy will.
  **Apothecary**
Put this in any liquid thing you will
And drink it off, and if you had the strength
Of twenty men, it would dispatch you straight.
  **Romeo**
80  There is thy gold, worse poison to men's souls,
Doing more murder in this loathsome world,
Than these poor compounds that thou mayst not sell.
I sell thee poison, thou hast sold me none.
Farewell, buy food, and get thyself in flesh.
                 [*Exit* Apothecary
85  Come, cordial and not poison, go with me
To Juliet's grave, for there must I use thee.    [*Exit*

## SCENE 2

*Verona: Friar Lawrence's cell. Enter* Friar John

  **Friar John**
Holy Franciscan friar, brother, ho!

*Enter* Friar Lawrence

  **Friar Lawrence**
This same should be the voice of Friar John.
Welcome from Mantua. What says Romeo?
Or if his mind be writ, give me his letter.
  **Friar John**
5  Going to find a barefoot brother out,
One of our order, to associate me,
Here in this city visiting the sick,
And finding him, the searchers of the town,
Suspecting that we both were in a house
10  Where the infectious pestilence did reign,
Seal'd up the doors, and would not let us forth,
So that my speed to Mantua there was stay'd.

**Friar Lawrence**

Who bare my letter then to Romeo?

**Friar John**

I could not send it—here it is again—

15 Nor get a messenger to bring it thee,

So fearful were they of infection.

**Friar Lawrence**

Unhappy fortune! By my brotherhood,

The letter was not nice but full of charge,

Of dear import, and the neglecting it

20 May do much danger. Friar John, go hence,

Get me an iron crow and bring it straight

Unto my cell.

**Friar John**

Brother, I'll go and bring it thee.                    [*Exit*

**Friar Lawrence**

Now must I to the monument alone,

25 Within this three hours will fair Juliet wake.

She will beshrew me much that Romeo

Hath had no notice of these accidents;

But I will write again to Mantua,

And keep her at my cell till Romeo come,

30 Poor living corse, clos'd in a dead man's tomb!       [*Exit*

## Scene 3

*Verona: a churchyard, with the tomb of the* Capulets.
*Enter* Paris *and his* Page *with flowers and sweet water
and torch*

**Paris**

Give me thy torch, boy. Hence, and stand aloof.

Yet put it out, for I would not be seen.

Under yond yew trees lay thee all along,

Holding thy ear close to the hollow ground,

5 So shall no foot upon the churchyard tread,

Being loose, unfirm with digging up of graves,

But thou shalt hear it. Whistle then to me

As signal that thou hear'st something approach.

Give me those flowers. Do as I bid thee, go.

---

18 *nice*: trivial.
*charge*: weighty matter.
19 *import*: importance.

21 *crow*: crowbar.
*straight*: immediately.

24 *must I*: I must go.

26 *beshrew*: curse.
27 *accidents*: happenings.

**Act 5 Scene 3**
Paris, praying at Juliet's tomb, encounters
Romeo; they fight, and Paris is killed. Friar
Lawrence is too late to save Romeo, who
swallows the poison he bought in Mantua,
and when Juliet sees his body she kills
herself. Friar Lawrence explains everything.

0s.d. *sweet*: scented.
1 *aloof*: at a distance.
2 *would not*: do not want to.
3 *all along*: on the ground.

10 *stand*: stay.

13 *canopy*: overhead covering (as on a
   four-poster bed).
14 *dew*: sprinkle.
15 *wanting*: lacking.
   *distill'd by*: extracted out of.
16 *obsequies*: funeral observances.

17s.d.  *Whistle Boy*: the Page must
   whistle.

19 *cursed*: cursèd.
20 *cross*: interfere with.

21s.d.  *mattock*: a kind of pickaxe.

26 *all aloof*: well away.
27 *my course*: what I intend to do.

30–1 *But . . . ring*: Romeo invents an
   excuse to mislead Balthasar.

32 *dear employment*: important business.
33 *jealous*: suspicious.

36 *hungry*: wanting more bodies.

**Page**
10 [*Aside*] I am almost afraid to stand alone
   Here in the churchyard, yet I will adventure.      [*Retires*

   Paris *strews the tomb with flowers*

**Paris**
   Sweet flower, with flowers thy bridal bed I strew—
   O woe, thy canopy is dust and stones!—
   Which with sweet water nightly I will dew,
15 Or wanting that, with tears distill'd by moans.
   The obsequies that I for thee will keep
   Nightly shall be to strew thy grave and weep.

   *Whistle* Boy

   The boy gives warning, something doth approach.
   What cursed foot wanders this way tonight,
20 To cross my obsequies and true love's rite?
   What, with a torch? Muffle me, night, a while.   [*Retires*

   *Enter* Romeo *and* Balthasar *with a torch, a mattock,
   and a crow of iron*

**Romeo**
   Give me that mattock and the wrenching iron.
   Hold, take this letter; early in the morning
   See thou deliver it to my lord and father.
25 Give me the light. Upon thy life I charge thee,
   What e'er thou hear'st or seest, stand all aloof,
   And do not interrupt me in my course.
   Why I descend into this bed of death
   Is partly to behold my lady's face,
30 But chiefly to take thence from her dead finger
   A precious ring, a ring that I must use
   In dear employment; therefore hence, be gone.
   But if thou, jealous, dost return to pry
   In what I farther shall intend to do,
35 By heaven, I will tear thee joint by joint,
   And strew this hungry churchyard with thy limbs.
   The time and my intents are savage-wild,

More fierce and more inexorable far
Than empty tigers or the roaring sea.

39 *empty*: hungry.

**Balthasar**

40 I will be gone, sir, and not trouble ye.

**Romeo**

So shalt thou show me friendship. Take thou that,

41 *So*: in this way.

*Gives a purse*

Live and be prosperous, and farewell, good fellow.

**Balthasar**

43 *For all this same*: despite what he
says.

[*Aside*] For all this same, I'll hide me hereabout,
His looks I fear, and his intents I doubt.        [*Retires*

**Romeo**

45 *maw*: stomach (i.e. the vault).

45 Thou detestable maw, thou womb of death,
Gorg'd with the dearest morsel of the earth,
Thus I enforce thy rotten jaws to open,

48 *in despite*: in defiance.
*more food*: i.e. his own body.

And in despite I'll cram thee with more food.

*Romeo begins to open the tomb*

**Paris**

This is that banish'd haughty Montague,
50 That murder'd my love's cousin, with which grief

51 *supposed*: supposèd.

It is supposed the fair creature died,
And here is come to do some villainous shame

53 *apprehend*: arrest.

To the dead bodies. I will apprehend him.

*Steps forth*

Stop thy unhallow'd toil, vile Montague!
55 Can vengeance be pursu'd further than death?

56 *Condemned*: condemnèd.

Condemned villain, I do apprehend thee.
Obey and go with me, for thou must die.

**Romeo**

I must indeed, and therefore came I hither.
Good gentle youth, tempt not a desp'rate man,

60 *these gone*: the dead bodies in the
churchyard.
61 *affright*: frighten.

60 Fly hence and leave me. Think upon these gone,
Let them affright thee. I beseech thee, youth,
Put not another sin upon my head,
By urging me to fury: O be gone!

By heaven, I love thee better than myself,
65 For I come hither arm'd against myself.
Stay not, be gone; live, and hereafter say,
A madman's mercy bid thee run away.
    **Paris**
I do defy thy conjuration,
And apprehend thee for a felon here.
    **Romeo**
70 Wilt thou provoke me? then have at thee, boy!

*They fight*

    **Page**
O Lord, they fight! I will go call the Watch.    [*Exit*
    **Paris**
O, I am slain! [*Falls*] If thou be merciful,
Open the tomb, lay me with Juliet. [*Dies*]
    **Romeo**
In faith, I will. Let me peruse this face.
75 Mercutio's kinsman, noble County Paris!
What said my man, when my betossed soul
Did not attend him as we rode? I think
He told me Paris should have married Juliet.
Said he not so? or did I dream it so?
80 Or am I mad, hearing him talk of Juliet,
To think it was so? O give me thy hand,
One writ with me in sour misfortune's book!
I'll bury thee in a triumphant grave.
A grave? O no, a lantern, slaughter'd youth;
85 For here lies Juliet, and her beauty makes
This vault a feasting presence full of light.
Death, lie thou there, by a dead man interr'd.

*Laying* Paris *in the tomb*

How oft when men are at the point of death
Have they been merry, which their keepers call
90 A light'ning before death! O how may I
Call this a light'ning? O my love, my wife,
Death, that hath suck'd the honey of thy breath,
Hath had no power yet upon thy beauty:

68 *defy thy conjuration*: reject your appeal.
69 *for a felon*: as a criminal.

76 *betossed*: betossèd; disturbed.
77 *attend*: listen to.

82 *writ with me*: whose name has been written with mine.
83 *triumphant*: magnificent (because it already holds Juliet).
84 *lantern*: a windowed turret on top of a cathedral or great hall.
86 *feasting presence*: festival reception-chamber.
87 *Death*: Romeo addresses the body of Paris, referring to himself as the 'dead man'.

89 *keepers*: prison warders, sickbed attendants.
90 *light'ning*: i.e. of the spirits.

94–6 *beauty's . . . there*: Perhaps Juliet is already recovering—or perhaps Shakespeare has forgotten that Friar Lawrence had said that 'The roses in thy lips and cheeks shall fade' (*4*, 1, 99).

94 *ensign*: flag; as long as beauty's red flag is seen in Juliet's cheeks and lips, the white flag of death cannot be raised ('advanced').

96 *advanced*: advancèd.

103 *unsubstantial*: bodiless.

104 *abhorred*: abhorrèd.

110 *set . . . rest*: make a final desperate commitment of myself.

111 *shake the yoke*: resist the domination. *inauspicious stars*: unfavourable Fortune.

114 *seal*: (a) close up; (b) make official. The legal imagery is continued in the next line.

Thou art not conquer'd, beauty's ensign yet
95 Is crimson in thy lips and in thy cheeks,
And death's pale flag is not advanced there.
Tybalt, liest thou there in thy bloody sheet?
O, what more favour can I do to thee
Than with that hand that cut thy youth in twain
100 To sunder his that was thine enemy?
Forgive me, cousin. Ah, dear Juliet,
Why art thou yet so fair? Shall I believe
That unsubstantial Death is amorous,
And that the lean abhorred monster keeps
105 Thee here in dark to be his paramour?
For fear of that, I still will stay with thee,
And never from this palace of dim night
Depart again. Here, here will I remain
With worms that are thy chambermaids; O here
110 Will I set up my everlasting rest,
And shake the yoke of inauspicious stars
From this world-wearied flesh. Eyes, look your last!
Arms, take your last embrace! and, lips, O you
The doors of breath, seal with a righteous kiss

'Come, bitter conduct, come, unsavoury guide!' (*5*, 3, 116). Ian McKellen as Romeo and Francesca Annis as Juliet, Royal Shakespeare Company, 1977.

115 *A dateless . . . Death*: an everlasting
contract with Death, who finally takes
possession of everything.
116 *conduct*: guide.
118 *bark*: small ship.

115 A dateless bargain to engrossing Death!
Come, bitter conduct, come, unsavoury guide!
Thou desperate pilot, now at once run on
The dashing rocks thy seasick weary bark!
Here's to my love! [*Drinks*] O true apothecary!
120 Thy drugs are quick. Thus with a kiss I die. [*Dies*]

*Enter* Friar Lawrence *with lantern, crow, and spade*

**Friar Lawrence**
Saint Francis be my speed! how oft tonight

121 *speed*: haste.
122 *stumbl'd at*: stumbled over; this was
regarded as a bad omen.

Have my old feet stumbl'd at graves! Who's there?
**Balthasar**
Here's one, a friend, and one that knows you well.
**Friar Lawrence**
Bliss be upon you! Tell me, good my friend,

125 *vainly*: in vain.

125 What torch is yond that vainly lends his light
To grubs and eyeless skulls? As I discern,

127 *Capels'*: Capulets'.

It burneth in the Capels' monument.
**Balthasar**
It doth so, holy sir, and there's my master,
One that you love.
**Friar Lawrence**                    Who is it?
**Balthasar**
                              Romeo.
**Friar Lawrence**
130 How long hath he been there?
**Balthasar**
                              Full half an hour.
**Friar Lawrence**
Go with me to the vault.
**Balthasar**
                    I dare not, sir.

132 *knows . . . hence*: thinks I have gone
away.

My master knows not but I am gone hence,
And fearfully did menace me with death
If I did stay to look on his intents.
**Friar Lawrence**
135 Stay then, I'll go alone. Fear comes upon me.

136 *ill unthrifty*: evil and unfortunate.

O, much I fear some ill unthrifty thing.

**Balthasar**
As I did sleep under this yew tree here,
I dreamt my master and another fought,
And that my master slew him.                    [*Retires*
    **Friar Lawrence**
                Romeo!

Friar *stoops and looks on the blood and weapons*

140 Alack, alack, what blood is this which stains
The stony entrance of this sepulchre?
What mean these masterless and gory swords
To lie discolour'd by this place of peace?

*Enters the tomb*

Romeo! O, pale! Who else? What, Paris too?
145 And steep'd in blood? Ah, what an unkind hour
Is guilty of this lamentable chance!

Juliet *rises*

The lady stirs.
    **Juliet**
O comfortable Friar, where is my lord?
I do remember well where I should be;
150 And there I am. Where is my Romeo?

*Noise within*

    **Friar Lawrence**
I hear some noise, lady. Come from that nest
Of death, contagion, and unnatural sleep.
A greater power than we can contradict
Hath thwarted our intents. Come, come away.
155 Thy husband in thy bosom there lies dead;
And Paris too. Come, I'll dispose of thee
Among a sisterhood of holy nuns.
Stay not to question, for the Watch is coming.
Come go, good Juliet, I dare no longer stay.    [*Exit*

142 *What mean*: why do.
    *masterless*: without owners.
143 *discolour'd*: unnaturally stained.

148 *comfortable*: providing spiritual
    comfort.

152 *unnatural sleep*: the sleep of death.

155 *in thy bosom*: Perhaps Juliet is still
    partly drugged, and doesn't realize
    that Romeo is lying across her body.

162 *timeless*: untimely.

163 *churl*: unmannerly peasant.

166 *a restorative*: the kiss that should have
     revived me.

169 *happy*: (a) fortunately placed;
     (b) successful.

173 *attach*: arrest.

176 *buried*: burièd.

**Juliet**

160 Go get thee hence, for I will not away.
     What's here? a cup clos'd in my true love's hand?
     Poison I see hath been his timeless end.
     O churl, drunk all, and left no friendly drop
     To help me after? I will kiss thy lips,
165 Haply some poison yet doth hang on them,
     To make me die with a restorative.
     Thy lips are warm.
          **Captain of the Watch**
     [*Within*] Lead, boy, which way?
          **Juliet**
     Yea, noise? Then I'll be brief. O happy dagger,

          *Taking* Romeo's *dagger*

170 This is thy sheath;

          *Stabs herself*

                    there rust, and let me die.

          *Falls on* Romeo's *body and dies*

          *Enter* Paris's *Boy and* Watch

          **Page**
     This is the place, there where the torch doth burn.
          **Captain of the Watch**
     The ground is bloody, search about the churchyard.
     Go, some of you, whoe'er you find attach.
                    [*Exeunt some of the* Watch

          *The* Captain *enters the tomb and returns*

     Pitiful sight! here lies the County slain,
175 And Juliet bleeding, warm, and newly dead,
     Who here hath lain this two days buried.
     Go tell the prince, run to the Capulets,
     Raise up the Montagues; some others search.
                    [*Exeunt others of the* Watch

179 *the ground*: the earth.

180 *the true ground*: the real cause.

181 *circumstance*: detailed knowledge.
    *descry*: perceive.

We see the ground whereon these woes do lie,
180 But the true ground of all these piteous woes
We cannot without circumstance descry.

*Enter one of the* Watch *with* Romeo's *man* Balthasar

**Second Watchman**
Here's Romeo's man, we found him in the churchyard.
    **Captain of the Watch**
Hold him in safety till the prince come hither.

*Enter* Friar Lawrence *and another* Watchman

**Third Watchman**
Here is a friar that trembles, sighs, and weeps.
185 We took this mattock and this spade from him,
As he was coming from this churchyard's side.
    **Captain of the Watch**
A great suspicion. Stay the friar too.

*Enter the* Prince *with others*

**Prince**
What misadventure is so early up,
That calls our person from our morning rest?

*Enter Capels,* Capulet, Lady Capulet

**Capulet**
190 What should it be that is so shriek'd abroad?
    **Lady Capulet**
O, the people in the street cry 'Romeo',
Some 'Juliet', and some 'Paris', and all run
With open outcry toward our monument.
    **Prince**
What fear is this which startles in your ears?
    **Captain of the Watch**
195 Sovereign, here lies the County Paris slain,
And Romeo dead, and Juliet, dead before,
Warm and new kill'd.

**Prince**
Search, seek, and know how this foul murder comes.
    **Captain of the Watch**
Here is a friar, and slaughter'd Romeo's man,
200 With instruments upon them, fit to open
These dead men's tombs.

*Capulet and* Lady Capulet *enter the tomb*

**Capulet**
O heavens! O wife, look how our daughter bleeds!
This dagger hath mistane, for lo his house
Is empty on the back of Montague,
205 And it mis-sheathed in my daughter's bosom!
    **Lady Capulet**
O me, this sight of death is as a bell
That warns my old age to a sepulchre.

*They return from the tomb*

*Enter* Montague

**Prince**
Come, Montague, for thou art early up
To see thy son and heir now early down.
    **Montague**
210 Alas, my liege, my wife is dead tonight;
Grief of my son's exile hath stopp'd her breath.
What further woe conspires against mine age?
    **Prince**
Look and thou shalt see.

*Montague enters the tomb and returns*

**Montague**
O thou untaught! what manners is in this,
215 To press before thy father to a grave?
    **Prince**
Seal up the mouth of outrage for a while,
Till we can clear these ambiguities,
And know their spring, their head, their true descent,

203 *house*: sheath.

205 *mis-sheathed*: mis-sheathèd.

207 *warns*: summons.

210 *is dead tonight*: died last night.

214 *untaught*: Montague's own death should have taught his son to die.
215 *press*: push.

216 *mouth of outrage*: your expressions of violent grief.

218 *spring*: source.

219 *general*: leader in your pursuit of justice.
220 *to death*: to get a death sentence on those who are guilty.
221 *let . . . patience*: let patience rule over misfortune.
222 *parties of suspicion*: suspects.
223 *greatest*: prime suspect.

225 *make*: argue.
226 *impeach*: accuse.
*purge*: clear from guilt.
227 *condemned*: condemnèd.

229 *my . . . breath*: the short time I have left to live.

233 *stol'n*: secretly snatched.

238 *perforce*: by force.

243 *tutor'd*: taught.

245 *wrought on*: produced in.
246 *form*: appearance.
247 *as*: on.

253 *prefixed*: prefixèd.

255 *closely*: secretly.

And then will I be general of your woes,
220 And lead you even to death. Mean time forbear,
And let mischance be slave to patience.
Bring forth the parties of suspicion.
    **Friar Lawrence**
I am the greatest, able to do least,
Yet most suspected, as the time and place
225 Doth make against me, of this direful murder;
And here I stand both to impeach and purge
Myself condemned and myself excus'd.
    **Prince**
Then say at once what thou dost know in this.
    **Friar Lawrence**
I will be brief, for my short date of breath
230 Is not so long as is a tedious tale.
Romeo, there dead, was husband to that Juliet,
And she, there dead, that Romeo's faithful wife:
I married them, and their stol'n marriage day
Was Tybalt's doomsday, whose untimely death
235 Banish'd the new-made bridegroom from this city,
For whom, and not for Tybalt, Juliet pin'd.
You, to remove that siege of grief from her,
Betroth'd and would have married her perforce
To County Paris. Then comes she to me,
240 And with wild looks bid me devise some mean
To rid her from this second marriage,
Or in my cell there would she kill herself.
Then gave I her (so tutor'd by my art)
A sleeping potion, which so took effect
245 As I intended, for it wrought on her
The form of death. Mean time I writ to Romeo
That he should hither come as this dire night
To help to take her from her borrow'd grave,
Being the time the potion's force should cease.
250 But he which bore my letter, Friar John,
Was stay'd by accident, and yesternight
Return'd my letter back. Then all alone,
At the prefixed hour of her waking,
Came I to take her from her kindred's vault,
255 Meaning to keep her closely at my cell,
Till I conveniently could send to Romeo.

But when I came, some minute ere the time
Of her awakening, here untimely lay
The noble Paris and true Romeo dead.
260 She wakes, and I entreated her come forth
And bear this work of heaven with patience.
But then a noise did scare me from the tomb,
And she too desperate would not go with me,
But as it seems, did violence on herself.
265 All this I know, and to the marriage

266 *is privy*: shared the secret.
267 *Miscarried*: went wrong.

Her nurse is privy; and if aught in this
Miscarried by my fault, let my old life
Be sacrific'd, some hour before his time,
Unto the rigour of severest law.
              **Prince**

270 *still*: always.

270 We still have known thee for a holy man.
Where's Romeo's man? what can he say to this?
              **Balthasar**
I brought my master news of Juliet's death,

273 *in post*: in haste.

And then in post he came from Mantua
To this same place, to this same monument.
275 This letter he early bid me give his father,

276 *going*: as he was going.

And threaten'd me with death, going in the vault,
If I departed not and left him there.
              **Prince**
Give me the letter, I will look on it.
Where is the County's page that rais'd the Watch?

280 *what . . . master*: what was your
master doing?

280 Sirrah, what made your master in this place?
              **Page**
He came with flowers to strew his lady's grave,
And bid me stand aloof, and so I did.

283 *Anon*: presently.

Anon comes one with light to ope the tomb,
And by and by my master drew on him,
285 And then I ran away to call the Watch.
              **Prince**
This letter doth make good the Friar's words,
Their course of love, the tidings of her death;
And here he writes that he did buy a poison
Of a poor pothecary, and therewithal
290 Came to this vault to die, and lie with Juliet.
Where be these enemies? Capulet, Montague?
See what a scourge is laid upon your hate,

294 *winking at*: closing my eyes to.

295 *a brace of kinsmen*: i.e. Mercutio and Paris.

297 *jointure*: dowry; all that Capulet can offer now is to join hands with Old Montague.

301 *figure*: statue. See Appendix, page 123.
*rate*: value.

303 *Romeo's*: i.e. Romeo's statue.
304 *sacrifices*: victims.

305 *glooming*: gloomy.

308 *punished*: punishèd.

That heaven finds means to kill your joys with love!
And I for winking at your discords too
295 Have lost a brace of kinsmen. All are punish'd.

**Capulet**
O brother Montague, give me thy hand.
This is my daughter's jointure, for no more
Can I demand.

**Montague**
⠀⠀⠀⠀⠀⠀⠀⠀But I can give thee more,
For I will raise her statue in pure gold,
300 That whiles Verona by that name is known,
There shall no figure at such rate be set
As that of true and faithful Juliet.

**Capulet**
As rich shall Romeo's by his lady's lie,
Poor sacrifices of our enmity!

**Prince**
305 A glooming peace this morning with it brings,
The sun for sorrow will not show his head.
Go hence to have more talk of these sad things;
Some shall be pardon'd, and some punished:
For never was a story of more woe
310 Than this of Juliet and her Romeo.⠀⠀⠀*[Exeunt omnes*

'Romeo, there dead, was husband to that Juliet, And she, there dead, that Romeo's faithful wife.' (*5*, 3, 231–2) David Waller as Friar Lawrence, Ivan Beavis as Montague, Barbara Shelley as Lady Capulet, John Woodvine as Capulet, Royal Shakespeare Company, 1976.

# Extracts from *Romeus and Juliet*
## by Arthur Brooke, 1562

*Act 1, Scenes 2–5*

The weary winter nights restore the Christmas games,
And now the season doth invite to banquet townish dames.
And first in Capel's house, the chief of all the kin,
Spar'th for no cost, the wonted use of banquets to begin.
No lady fair or foul was in Verona town,
No knight or gentleman of high or low renown,
But Capulet himself hath bid unto his feast,
Or by his name in paper sent, appointed as a guest.
Young damsels thither flock, of bachelors a rout,
Not so much for the banquet's sake, as beauties to search out.
But not a Montague would enter at his gate—
For, as you heard, the Capulets and they were at debate—
Save Romeus, and he in mask with hidden face,
The supper done, with other five, did press into the place.
When they had masqu'd a while, with dames in courtly wise,
All did unmask, the rest did show them to their ladies' eyes.
But bashful Romeus with shamefast face forsook
The open press, and him withdrew into the chamber's nook.
But brighter than the sun, the waxen torches shone,
That maugre what he could, he was espied of everyone. ...
The Capulets disdain the presence of their foe,
Yet they suppress their stirred ire, the cause I do not know.
Perhaps t'offend their guests the courteous knights are loth,
Perhaps they stay from sharp revenge, dreading the Prince's wrath;
Perhaps for that they sham'd to exercise their rage
Within their house, 'gainst one alone, and him of tender age.

(lines 155–172, 183–188)

*Act 1, Scene 5*

As careful was the maid what way were best devise
To learn his name, that entertain'd her in so gentle wise,
Of whom her heart receiv'd so deep, so wide a wound.
An ancient dame she call'd to her, and in her ear gan round.

This old dame in her youth had nurs'd her with her milk,
With slender needle taught her sew, and how to spin with silk.
'What twain are those,' quoth she, 'which press unto the door,
Whose pages in their hand do bear two torches' light before?'
And then as each of them had of his household name,
So she him nam'd yet once again, the young and wily dame.
'And tell me who is he with visor in his hand,
That yonder doth in masquing weed beside the window stand?'
'His name is Romeus,' said she, 'a Montague,
Whose father's pride first stirr'd the strife which both your households
    rue.'
The word of 'Montague' her joys did overthrow,
And straight instead of happy hope, despair began to grow.
'What hap have I,' quoth she, 'to love my father's foe?
What, am I weary of my weal? What, do I wish my woe?'

(lines 341–358)

### Act 4, Scene 3

'What do I know,' quoth she, 'if that this powder shall
Sooner or later than it should, or else not work at all?
And then my craft descried as open as the day,
The people's tale and laughing stock shall I remain for aye?'
'And what know I,' quoth she, 'if serpents odious,
And other beasts and worms that are of nature venomous,
That wonted are to lurk in dark cave underground,
And commonly (as I have heard) in dead men's tombs are found,
Shall harm me—yea or nay—where I shall lie as dead?
Or how shall I, that always have in so fresh air been bred,
Endure the loathsome stink of such an heaped store
Of carcasses not yet consum'd, and bones that long before
Entombed were, where I my sleeping-place shall have
Where all my ancestors do rest, my kindred's common grave?
Shall not the friar and my Romeus, when they come,
Find me (if I awake before) y-stifled in the tomb?'
    And whilst she in these thoughts doth dwell somewhat too long,
The force of her imagining anon did wax so strong
That she surmis'd she saw out of the hollow vault
(A grisly thing to look upon) the carcass of Tybalt. . . .
Her dainty tender parts gan shiver all for dread,
Her golden hairs did stand upright upon her chillish head.

Then pressed with the fear that she there lived in,
A sweat as cold as mountain ice pierc'd through her tender skin,
That with the moisture hath wet every part of hers,
And more besides, she vainly thinks, whilst vainly thus she fears,
A thousand bodies dead have compass'd her about,
And lest they will dismember her, she greatly stands in doubt.
But when she felt her strength began to wear away,
By little and little, and in her heart her fear increased aye,
Dreading that weakness might, or foolish cowardice,
Hinder the execution of the purpos'd enterprise,
As she had frantic been, in haste the glass she caught.
And up she drank the mixture quite, without further thought.

(lines 2361–2380, 2387–2400)

### Act 4, Scene 1

Now throughout Italy this common use they have,
That all the best of every stock are earthed in one grave,
For every household, if it be of any fame,
Doth build a tomb or dig a vault that bears the household's name;
Wherein (if any of that kindred hap to die)
They are bestow'd, else in the same no other corpse may lie.
The Capulets her corpse in such a one did lay,
Where Tybalt, slain of Romeus, was laid the other day.
An other use there is, that whosoever dies,
Born to the church with open face, upon the bier he lies
In wonted weeds attir'd, not wrapp'd in winding-sheet.

(lines 2515–2525)

### Act 5, Scene 3

And lest that length of time might from our minds remove
The memory of so perfect, sound, and so approved love,
The bodies dead removed from the vault where they did die,
In stately tomb, on pillars great, of marble raise they high.
On every side above were set—and eke beneath—
Great store of cunning epitaphs, in honour of their death.
And even at this day the tomb is to be seen,
So that among the monuments that in Verona been,
There is no monument more worthy of the sight
Than is the tomb of Juliet, and Romeus her knight.

(lines 3011–3020)

# *Background*

## England in 1595

When Shakespeare was writing *Romeo and Juliet*, many people still believed that the sun went round the earth. They were taught that this was the way God had ordered things, and that – in England – God had founded a Church and appointed a Monarchy so that the land and people could be well governed.

'The past is a foreign country; they do things differently there.'

L. P. Hartley

### Government

For most of Shakespeare's life, the reigning monarch of England was Queen Elizabeth I. With her counsellors and ministers, she governed the nation from London, although fewer than half a million people out of a total population of six million lived in the capital city. In the rest of the country, law and order were maintained by the land-owners and enforced by their deputies. The average man had no vote, and women had no rights at all.

### Religion

At this time, England was a Christian country. All children were baptized, soon after they were born, into the Church of England; they were taught the essentials of the Christian faith, and instructed in their duty to God and to humankind. Marriages and funerals were conducted only by the licensed clergy and according to the Church's rites and ceremonies. Attending divine service was compulsory; absences (without a good medical reason) could be punished by fines. By such means, the authorities were able to keep some control over the population – recording births, marriages, and deaths; being alert to anyone who refused to accept standard religious practices, who could be politically dangerous; and ensuring that people received the approved teachings through the official 'Homilies' which were regularly preached in all parish churches.

Elizabeth I's father, Henry VIII, had broken away from the

Church of Rome, and from that time all people in England were able to hear the church services *in their own language* rather than in Latin. The Book of Common Prayer was used in every church, and an English translation of the Bible was read aloud in public. The Christian religion had never been so well taught before!

## Education

School education reinforced the Church's teaching. From the age of four, boys might attend the 'petty school' (its name came from the French '*petite école*') to learn reading and writing along with a few prayers; some schools also included work with numbers. At the age of seven, the boy was ready for the grammar school (if his father was willing and able to pay the fees).

Grammar schools taught Latin grammar, translation work and the study of Roman authors, paying attention as much to style as to content. The art of fine writing was therefore important from early youth. A very few students went on to university; these were either clever boys who won scholarships, or else the sons of rich noblemen. Girls stayed at home, and learned domestic and social skills – cooking, sewing, perhaps even music. The lucky ones might learn to read and write.

## Language

At the start of the sixteenth century the English had a very poor opinion of their own language: there was little serious writing in English, and hardly any literature. Latin was the language of international scholarship, and the eloquent style of the Romans was much admired. Many translations from Latin were made, and in this way writers increased the vocabulary of English and made its grammar more flexible. French, Italian, and Spanish works were also translated and, for the first time, there were English versions of the Bible. By the end of the century, English was a language to be proud of: it was rich in vocabulary, capable of infinite variety and subtlety, and ready for all kinds of word-play – especially *puns*, for which Elizabethan English is renowned.

## Drama

The great art-form of the Elizabethan and Jacobean age was its drama. The Elizabethans inherited a tradition of play-acting from the Middle Ages, and they reinforced this by reading and translating the Roman playwrights. At the beginning of the sixteenth century plays were performed by groups of actors. These were all-male companies (boys acted the female roles) who travelled from town to town, setting up their stages in open places (such as inn-yards) or, with the permission of the owner, in the hall of some noble house. The touring companies continued outside London into the seventeenth century; but in London, in 1576, a new building was erected for the performance of plays. This was the Theatre, the first purpose-built playhouse in England. Other playhouses followed, including the Globe, where most of Shakespeare's plays were performed, and English drama reached new heights.

There were people who disapproved, of course. The theatres, which brought large crowds together, could encourage the spread of disease – and dangerous ideas. During the summer, when the plague was at its worst, the playhouses were closed. A constant censorship was imposed, more or less severe at different times. The Puritans, a religious and political faction who wanted to impose strict rules of behaviour, tried to close down the theatres. However, partly because the royal family favoured drama, and partly because the buildings were outside the city limits, they did not succeed until 1642.

## Theatre

From contemporary comments and sketches – most particularly a drawing by a Dutch visitor, Johannes de Witt – it is possible to form some idea of the typical Elizabethan playhouse for which most of Shakespeare's plays were written. Hexagonal (six-sided) in shape, it had three roofed galleries encircling an open courtyard. The plain, high stage projected into the yard, where it was surrounded by the audience of standing 'groundlings'. At the back were two doors for the actors' entrances and exits; and above these doors was a balcony – useful for a musicians' gallery or for the acting of scenes '*above*'. Over the stage was a thatched roof, supported on two pillars, forming a canopy – which seems to have been painted with the sun, moon, and stars for the 'heavens'.

Underneath was space (concealed by curtains) which could be used by characters ascending and descending through a trap-door in the stage. Costumes and properties were kept backstage in the 'tiring house'. The actors used the most luxurious costumes they could find, often clothes given to them by rich patrons. Stage properties were important for showing where a scene was set, but the dramatist's own words were needed to explain the time of day, since all performances took place in the early afternoon.

A replica of Shakespeare's own theatre, the Globe, has been built in London, and stands in Southwark, almost exactly on the Bankside site of the original.

Shakespeare's Globe, Southwark, London, England.

# *William Shakespeare, 1564–1616*

Elizabeth I was Queen of England when Shakespeare was born in 1564. He was the son of a tradesman who made and sold gloves in the small town of Stratford-upon-Avon, and he was educated at the grammar school in that town. Shakespeare did not go to university when he left school, but worked, perhaps, in his father's business. When he was eighteen he married Anne Hathaway, who became the mother of his daughter, Susanna, in 1583, and of twins in 1585.

There is nothing exciting, or even unusual, in this story; and from 1585 until 1592 there are no documents that can tell us anything at all about Shakespeare. But we have learned that in 1592 he was known in London, and that he had become both an actor and a playwright.

We do not know when Shakespeare wrote his first play, and we are not sure of the order in which he wrote his works. If you look on page 131 at the list of his writings and their approximate dates, you will see he started by writing plays on subjects taken from the history of England. No doubt this was partly because he was patriotic and interested in English history, but he was also a very shrewd businessman. He could see that the theatre audiences enjoyed being shown their own history, and it was certain that he would make a profit from this kind of drama.

He also wrote comedies, with romantic love-stories of young people who fall in love with one another, and at the end of the play marry and live happily ever after.

At the end of the sixteenth century Shakespeare wrote some melancholy, bitter, and tragic plays. This change may have been caused by some sadness in the writer's life (his only son died in 1596). Shakespeare, however, was not the only writer whose works at this time were very serious. The whole of England was facing a crisis. Queen Elizabeth I was growing old. She was greatly loved, and the people were sad to think she must soon die; they were also afraid, because the queen had never married, and so there was no child to succeed her.

When James I, Elizabeth's Scottish cousin, came to the throne in 1603, Shakespeare continued to write serious drama—the great tragedies and the plays based on Roman history (such as *Julius Caesar*) for which he is most famous. Finally, before he retired from the theatre, he wrote another set of comedies. These all have the same theme: they tell of happiness which is lost, and then found again.

Shakespeare returned from London to Stratford, his home town. He was rich and successful, and he owned one of the biggest houses in the town. He died in 1616.

Shakespeare also wrote two long poems, and a collection of sonnets. The sonnets describe two love affairs, but we do not know who the lovers were – or whether they existed only in Shakespeare's imagination. Although there are many public documents concerned with his career as a writer and a businessman, Shakespeare has hidden his personal life from us. A nineteenth-century poet, Matthew Arnold, addressed Shakespeare in a poem, and wrote 'We ask and ask – Thou smilest, and art still'.

There is not even a portrait of the world's greatest dramatist that we can be sure is really of Shakespeare, and painted by someone who had seen him.

# Approximate Dates of Composition of Shakespeare's Works

| Period | Comedies | History plays | Tragedies | Poems |
|---|---|---|---|---|
| I<br>before 1594 | Comedy of Errors<br>Taming of the Shrew<br>Two Gentlemen of Verona<br>Love's Labour's Lost | Henry VI, part 1<br>Henry VI, part 2<br>Henry VI, part 3<br>Richard III | Titus Andronicus | Venus and Adonis<br>Rape of Lucrece |
| II<br>1594 – 1599 | Midsummer Night's Dream<br>Merchant of Venice<br>Merry Wives of Windsor<br>Much Ado About Nothing<br>As You Like It | Richard II<br>King John<br>Henry IV, part 1<br>Henry IV, part 2<br>Henry V | Romeo and Juliet | Sonnets |
| III<br>1599 – 1608 | Twelfth Night<br>Troilus and Cressida<br>Measure for Measure<br>All's Well That Ends Well<br>Pericles | | Julius Caesar<br>Hamlet<br>Othello<br>Timon of Athens<br>King Lear<br>Macbeth<br>Antony and Cleopatra<br>Coriolanus | |
| IV<br>1608 – 1613 | Cymbeline<br>The Winter's Tale<br>The Tempest | Henry VIII | | |

# Exploring *Romeo and Juliet* in the Classroom

Not only is it the world's most famous love story, but because this play delves into fiery passions and tempers, the complications of friendship and enmity, and how teenagers become independent of their parents, it speaks to young people like no other.

This section suggests a range of approaches in the classroom, to help bring the text to life and to engender both enjoyment and understanding of the play.

## Ways into the Play

Students may feel an antipathy towards the study of Shakespeare. The imaginative and enthusiastic teacher, with the help of this edition of the play, will soon break this down!

**Pictures**

Every picture tells a story, so ask your students to look at the picture on the front cover of this book and guess who the people are and what is happening. Once they are more familiar with the play, ask them to hazard a guess as to the exact moment in the play that is depicted.

This is a play about the fickleness of fate and love. Provide a selection of photographs of young men and women (e.g. from magazines) and ask your students to take on the role of Fate and match up the pictures to make couples. Perhaps they could then tell the story and predict the destiny of the couple they have brought together.

**Navigating the play**

Your students may need some help and practice at finding their way around a Shakespeare play. After explaining the division into acts, scenes and lines, challenge them to look up some references as quickly as possible. Refer them to some of the famous lines and those that might lead on to further discussion of the plot. Below are some suggestions.

The Prologue, line 6          *A pair of star-cross'd lovers take their life*

Act I, Scene i, line 169          *Here's much to do with hate, but more with love*

| | |
|---|---|
| Act II, Scene ii, line 33 | *O Romeo, Romeo, wherefore art thou Romeo?* |
| Act III, Scene v, lines 114–5 | *The County Paris, at Saint Peter's Church, Shall happily make thee there a joyful bride.* |

**Improvisation**

Working on one of these improvisations may help students to access some of the ideas behind the drama.

a) An improvisation involving two friends. One friend is fed up and unhappy (the students will need to decide why). The other friend is trying to persuade him or her to go to a party. The first friend does not want to go, nor does he or she have an invitation. What happens?

b) An improvisation involving a parent and teenage son or daughter. The parent has arranged a really good holiday for the next week. It's a very expensive holiday, and so the teenager should be pleased. However, he or she has made other arrangements (e.g. a job interview, a first date). The teenager doesn't want to go on the holiday, but they can't tell the parent why because the parent won't approve. What happens?

c) An improvisation of a conversation in which one person is angry and unhappy with the other, who nevertheless remains calm, friendly and placatory. Ask the pairs to swap over roles, and then discuss how it felt to be in each role.

## Setting the Scene

**The Prologue**

The use of a Chorus was a familiar element of classical theatre. Shakespeare provides a one-man Chorus to introduce the play and summarize the plot.

Create a cloze exercise, using the Prologue. Extract various key words into a word bank and then ask your students to put them back into the right place. This will encourage them to read the Prologue for meaning, before you read it through together.

Alternatively, ask your students to use the Prologue to find answers to the 5Ws: What? Who? Where? When? Why? Encourage them to find as many answers as they can to each question.

Discuss why Shakespeare used a Prologue to reveal the whole plot, and the benefits and disadvantages of doing so.

**Opposites attract**

This is a play full of opposites and contrasts: love and hate, peace and conflict, young and old. Explore the idea of opposites by giving your students various words (e.g. love, friend, heavy, cold, dark, chaos) and asking them to find antonyms for each one. Ask them to spot the use of opposites as they read the play.

**Families and feuds**

The cause of the feud between the two families has long been forgotten. However, it has been perpetuated and affects not just the families, but those around them. (Neither Mercutio nor Paris are related to either family but both lose their lives because of the feud.) Even the servants fight for their masters.

Your students will probably find it helpful to be introduced to the families and the main players before they read the play. Using the character names and descriptions (see pages ix–x), create a puzzle whereby the students match the names to the descriptions. They can follow this up by creating a diagram – a sort of family tree – showing the families and those close to them.

## Keeping Track of the Action

It's important to give your students opportunities to 'digest' and reflect upon their reading, so that they can take ownership of the play.

**Reading journals**

As you read through the play, help your students to trace and understand the plot by asking them to keep a journal each, in which they record what happens. They can also record their reactions and thoughts about the action and the characters. Their responses can be kept focused through specific questions from the teacher. As part of their journal, they can keep a timeline, which charts the main events of the play over the course of the five days, from Sunday to Thursday.

**Storybording**

Marcia Williams (see 'Further Reading and Resources', page 140) has created colourful and engaging cartoon versions of some of Shakespeare's plays. Cartoon strip versions of scenes can be helpful for younger students in particular. Give them an example (perhaps through looking at a page of Williams' version) of how to sum up the action in pictures, captions (explaining what is happening) and speech/thought bubbles (for key words and lines). Then ask them to complete their own storyboard for the scene being studied. Ideas for suitable scenes are:

| | |
|---|---|
| Act v, Scene v | (the Capulets' feast, including the first meeting of Romeo and Juliet) |
| Act iii, Scene iii | (the fights between Tybalt and Mercutio, and Tybalt and Romeo) |
| Act v, Scene iii | (the deaths of Romeo and Juliet) |

**Horoscopes**    The play follows the fortunes of the 'star-cross'd lovers'. Their fate seems to be in the stars. Your students can write horoscopes for different characters at various points in the action. Some suggestions are:

| | |
|---|---|
| Act i, Scene iii | (Juliet – marriage is in the air) |
| Act i, Scene v | (Romeo – looks for love and finds it unexpectedly) |
| Act ii, Scenes iv and v | (the Nurse – exciting developments with a loved one) |
| Act iii, Scene i | (Mercutio and Tybalt – the future is uncertain) |
| Act iv, Scene i | (Friar Lawrence – a favour to a friend may not turn out as planned) |

Ideally the horoscopes should have some ambiguity, reflecting both the students' grasp of the plot, the characters and the fickle finger of fate.

**Film versions**    The two film versions of *Romeo and Juliet*, directed by Zeffirelli and Luhrmann, provide excellent opportunities for your students to engage with performances of the play. Exploring different interpretations and treatments can give real insight into the drama. Students can compare the directors' treatments of the setting, individual characters such as the Prince, or individual scenes such as the balcony scene.

Looking at such aspects as filming techniques, music, and costumes can stimulate students to create their own interpretations. For example, they could be challenged to design a futuristic version of the Capulets' party or the sword fight, including music, special effects, etc.

DVD versions mean that effective stills can be captured and analysed, giving even greater insight into the filmmakers' skills.

GCSE students may be able to develop this into a piece of coursework that examines a director's interpretation of the play (or part of the play).

## Characters

Students of all ages need to come to an understanding of the characters: their motivations, their relationships, and their development.

**Masks**

Romeo is able to gatecrash the Capulets' party because he is wearing a mask. Explain that masquerades were popular when the play was written. Ask your students to design a mask for one of the characters in the play. The mask should reveal something of the chosen character's personality.

**Txt**

At the Capulet party, Romeo and Juliet fall in love at first sight. Challenge your students to capture the suddenness and ease of events, as well as the strength of their feelings, in a brief text message from Romeo or Juliet to someone they trust. Juliet might text her nurse, for example, whilst Romeo texts Friar Lawrence. The students could also compose the reply.

**A different perspective**

Allowing your students the opportunity to think, write, and talk as one of the characters, gives them a new and illuminating perspective on the character(s). Here are some possible scenarios.

a) Prince Escales writes an official report on the deaths of Tybalt and Mercutio (Act III, Scene i).

b) Lady Capulet is full of emotion because of the death of Tybalt and the attitude of her daughter (Act III, Scene v). Write her thoughts in her diary.

c) Imagine that Juliet records a video diary before she takes the potion. What would she say to her parents?

**Obituary**

Explain the purpose and conventions of an obituary and if possible show one from a newspaper. Ask your students to write an obituary for one of the characters who dies in the play, e.g. Mercutio, Juliet, or Paris.

# Themes

There are many themes and ideas running through the play and they often come in pairs, e.g. love and hate, friendship and enmity, youth and age. Here are just a few ways to explore them.

**Question and answer**  Take one theme or idea and ask your students to compose up to five questions related to that theme. For example, on the theme of love, students might ask, 'Isn't Juliet too young to be really in love?' or 'How can we be sure Romeo's love is genuine when he falls in love so quickly after Rosaline rejects him?' Students should swap their questions with a partner and attempt to answer the partner's questions. Any that are too difficult can be thrown open to the class.

**Theme collage**  Give your students a theme from the play (or a pair of themes, such as friendship and enmity) and ask them to create a pictorial representation of the theme in the modern world, using pictures, photographs, colours, words, and quotations from *Romeo and Juliet*.

**Judge a book by its cover**  Ask your students to design a new cover for this book or a programme for a performance of the play, which reveals something of the themes of the play as well as giving the essential information.

**Being a teenager**  In the play, Juliet moves from being a submissive and obedient daughter to being an independent and wilful one, who deceives her parents. Discuss whether this is credible and realistic. How does it fit your students' own experiences of being teenagers? What would Juliet write to an agony aunt? Ask your students to write the letter and the reply.

# Shakespeare's Language

**Sonnets**  Shakespeare exploits the sonnet form in *Romeo and Juliet*, notably using it when the lovers first meet (Act 1, Scene v, lines 92FF). Remind your students of the key features of a sonnet: 14 lines, 3 quatrains, a final rhyming couplet. Encourage them to explore the cleverness with which Shakespeare uses the sonnet at this significant point in the play and how the lovers' lines intertwine as they fall in love. Explore, too, how the religious imagery emphasizes the depth and seriousness of their emotions.

The students may even create their own poetry – a modern sonnet on the theme of love, some rhyming couplets, or the lyrics for a song using ideas from *Romeo and Juliet*. James Muirden's *Shakespeare in a Nutshell* (see 'Further Reading and Resources, page 140) gives a rhyming version of the whole play that you might like to share with your class.

**Oxymorons**

The love-struck Romeo is particularly well versed in the use of the oxymoron. Commenting on the recent conflict, and embroiled in his own private misery, his speech in Act 1, Scene 1, lines 165ff contains a string of opposites, '…Feather of lead, bright smoke, cold fire, sick health…' and so on. Discuss the effect of this feature and challenge your students to create their own oxymorons, either on a theme from the play (such as youth, friendship) or a subject of their own choosing (e.g. nature, cars, or teachers).

**Insults**

Ask your students to find some of the insults in the play, e.g. 'biting the thumb', 'slave', 'dog', 'coward'. Of particular significance is the word 'villain'. Tybalt repeatedly tries to bait Romeo with it. Encourage your students to investigate the effect of this word, what Tybalt intends when he uses it, and how it could be spoken. The students might collate a list of synonyms that echo the word 'villain' and the feelings Tybalt has for Romeo, or else might devise an acrostic poem, using the letters from 'villain', which reveals Tybalt's intentions behind using the word.

## Exploring with Drama

Book the hall or push back the desks because the best way to study a great play is through drama. Students of all ages will benefit from a dramatic encounter with *Romeo and Juliet*. They will enjoy the opportunity to act out a scene or two, or to explore the situations through improvisation, e.g. putting a character in the 'hot seat' for questioning by others.

**A ball and masquerade**

A good way to enter the spirit of Shakespeare's own times is for students to create their own formal Elizabethan dance steps. With some appropriate sixteenth-century music and, ideally, a glimpse at the Zeffirelli film version of the ball, ask small groups to choreograph their own dance. When you are ready to hold the party, each group must teach their dance to the rest of the class. Masks might also be designed, made, and worn.

**Conscience corridor**    Romeo and Juliet both act impulsively. But what would have happened if they had thought some of their decisions through first? Choose a significant part of the play for one of them (e.g. when Juliet decides to fake her suicide) and create a conscience corridor for them. One student will play Juliet and the rest of the class will create two lines facing each other, forming the corridor. One side of the corridor will advise caution and the other side of the corridor will urge her to go on with her plan. Juliet must walk down the corridor to seek advice. As she passes, each student will urge her to take their guidance. Once she reaches the end, she must decide what to do.

**The inquest**    Create the inquest that might take place at the end of this tragedy. Give character parts out to some students, whilst the rest must act as jury or television reporters. The Prince, presiding, will interview each of the remaining characters as to their actions, their motivations, and their assessment of what has happened. The reporters will take notes.

At the end of the inquest, the jury must discuss and decide who is to blame. The reporters must rehearse their TV reports. Finally the jury and journalists present their conclusions.

## Writing about *Romeo and Juliet*

If your students have to write about Romeo or Juliet for coursework or for examinations, you may wish to give them this general guidance.

- Read the question or task carefully, highlight the key words, and answer all parts of the question.
- Planning is essential. Plan what will be in each paragraph. You can change your plan if necessary.
- Avoid retelling the story.
- *Romeo and Juliet* is a play, so consider the impact or effect on the audience.
- Use the Point, Evidence, Explanation (PEE) structure to explain points.
- Adding Evaluation (PEEE!) will gain you higher marks.
- Keep quotations short.
- Avoid referring to a film version of the play, unless this is part of your task.

# Further Reading and Resources

### General

Fantasia, Louis, *Instant Shakespeare: a practical guide for actors, directors and teachers* (A & C Black, 2002)

Greer, Germaine, *Shakespeare: a very short introduction* (Oxford, 2002)

Hall, Peter, *Shakespeare's Advice to the Players* (Oberon Books, 2003)

Holden, Anthony, *Shakespeare: his life and work* (Abacus, 2002)

Kneen, Judith, *Teaching Shakespeare from Transition to Test* (Oxford University Press, 2004)

McConnell, Louise, *Exit, Pursued by a Bear – Shakespeare's characters, plays, poems, history and stagecraft* (Bloomsbury, 2003)

McLeish and Unwin, *A Pocket Guide to Shakespeare's Plays* (Faber and Faber, 1998)

Muirden, James, *Shakespeare in a Nutshell: A Rhyming Guide to All the Plays* (Constable, 2004)

Wood, Michael, *In Search of Shakespeare* (BBC, 2003)


### Children's/students' books

Carpenter, Humphrey, *Shakespeare Without the Boring Bits* (Viking, 1994)

Deary, Terry, *Top Ten Shakespeare Stories* (Scholastic, 1998)

Ganeri, Anita, *What they don't tell you about Shakespeare* (Hodder, 1996)

Garfield, Leon, *Shakespeare Stories* (Puffin, 1997)

Garfield, Leon, *Shakespeare: The Animated Tales* (Egmont, 2002)

Lamb, Charles and Mary, *Tales from Shakespeare* (Puffin, 1987)

McCaughrean, Geraldine, *Stories from Shakespeare* (Orion, 1997)

Williams, Marcia, *Mr William Shakespeare's Plays* (Walker, 2000)

## Websites

*The Complete Works of Shakespeare*
http://the-tech.mit.edu/Shakespeare/

*Elizabethan pronunciation*
Includes information on insults.
http://www.renfaire.com/Language/index.html

Encyclopaedia Britannica – *Shakespeare and the Globe: Then and Now*
Information about the Globe and the theatre in Shakespeare's times.
http://search.eb.com/shakespeare/index2.html

*The Royal Shakespeare Company website*
As well as information on the theatre company, there are resources on the plays and the life and times of Shakespeare.
http://www.rsc.org.uk/home/index.asp

*The Shakespeare Birthplace Trust*
Information on his works, life, and times.
http://www.shakespeare.org.uk/homepage

*Shakespeare's Globe*
Information on the Globe Theatre, London.
http://www.shakespeares-globe.org/

*Shakespeare Illustrated*
An excellent source of paintings and pictures based on Shakespeare's plays.
http://www.emory.edu/ENGLISH/classes/Shakespeare_Illustrated/Shakespeare.html

*Spark Notes: A Midsummer Night's Dream*
An online study guide.
http://www.sparknotes.com/shakespeare/msnd/

*Mr William Shakespeare and the Internet*
A comprehensive guide to Shakespeare resources on the Internet.
http://shakespeare.palomar.edu/

### *Film, video, DVD, and audio*

Romeo and Juliet
Directed by Franco Zeffirelli (1968)

Romeo and Juliet
Directed by Baz Luhrmann (1996)

Shakespeare: Romeo and Juliet (audio CD)
BBC Radio Collection (1999)